Mastering the Art of Q & A:
A Survival Guide for Tough, Trick, and Hostile Questions

Mastering the Art of Q & A:
A Survival Guide for Tough, Trick, and Hostile Questions

Myles Martel, Ph.D.

DOW JONES-IRWIN
Homewood, Illinois 60430

This publication is designed to provide accurate and authoritative information in regard to the subject matter covered. It is sold with the understanding that neither the author nor the publisher is engaged in rendering legal, accounting, or other professional service. If legal advice or other expert assistance is required, the services of a competent professional person should be sought.

From a Declaration of Principles jointly adopted by a Committee of the American Bar Association and a Committee of Publishers.

Sponsoring editor: Jim Childs
Project editor: Joan Hopkins
Production manager: Carma W. Fazio
Production services: Editing, Design & Production, Inc.
Jacket Design: Michael Finkelman
Compositor: TCSystems, Inc.
Typeface: 11/13 Century Schoolbook
Printer: Semline/Book Press

LIBRARY OF CONGRESS
Library of Congress Cataloging-in-Publication Data

Martel, Myles.
    Mastering the art of Q and A : a survival guide for tough, trick and hostile questions / Myles Martel.
      p.   cm.
    Bibliography: p.
    Includes index.
    ISBN 1-556-23141-5
    1. Communication in management.   2. Questions and answers.
I. Title.
HD30.3.M374 1989
658.4′52—dc19

88–21763
CIP

Printed in the United States of America

1 2 3 4 5 6 7 8 9 0 B P 5 4 2 1 0 9 8

To my wife, Susan, who encouraged me to return temporarily to the life of an author; to David, our 10-year-old son, who has already mastered the art of questioning; and to the memory of a mortal whose immortal teachings spawned my interest in this subject—Socrates.

Acknowledgments

One author's name on the cover hardly does justice to the large number of people who help make any book, including *Mastering the Art of Q & A*, a reality.

Special appreciation is extended to:

Andrew Kurtz, my research assistant, for his superlative work, warm friendship, and good humor.

Irv Rockwood, my literary agent, for his impressively attentive and extremely helpful guidance.

Jim Childs, my editor, for his valuable editorial insights and total support from day one.

Jean Reagan, my secretary, for skillfully preparing the manuscript and tolerating my endless revisions with enviable patience and grace.

Peggy Ruggiero, my executive assistant, for running Martel & Associates smoothly while I went into hiding to write this book.

Carolyn Keefe and John Vlandis, my colleagues and long-time friends who, as always, provided numerous valuable insights.

Contents

PART V

Introduction

A Wall Street firm recently selected my firm to prepare a group of its executives for a major sales conference. The person who chose us told me forthrightly, "We're not worried about their presentations; our main concern is how they handle Q & A."

His concern was astute. Although he had assembled an impressive team of presenters, he realized that executives seldom devote sufficient preparation time to Q & A—even though the Q & A session can be more important than the presentation.

The Q & A exchange can be more significant than the presentation for four principal reasons.

1. It automatically stimulates a more direct sense of involvement with the audience.
2. It is usually more relevant than the presentation, especially since each answer is directly keyed to a concern or interest reflected in the audience member's question.
3. It tends to project more authenticity—and therefore more credibility—than a carefully preplanned presentation.
4. The dynamics of the Q & A interaction—including the climate of challenge and conflict—often make the Q & A more attention-getting and interesting than the presentation.

Regardless of whether the setting you are preparing for is a sales conference, public speech, media interview, government hearing, or job interview, the quality of the Q & A exchange can make the difference between success and failure. And because the Q & A is usually not a set, fully scripted piece, it can introduce a wide range of risks, particularly:

1. Not knowing an answer to an important question
2. Making a misstatement or gaffe
3. Projecting an improper image
4. Being caught in an awkward stall
5. Losing composure
6. Being perceived as unclear
7. Being perceived as boring
8. Being perceived as unresponsive
9. Overanswering or underanswering a question
10. Talking above or below the audience
11. Stepping into a trap
12. Missing important opportunities to present key messages

These risks are accentuated in high-stakes situations such as major presentations and media interviews. In fact, many executives who now rely on our counsel had been totally unwilling to interact with the media because of their fear of how a misstatement or poor performance could impede—or destroy—their career paths. Yet ironically, the career paths of so many of them were already being impeded because of their unwillingness to face the media and capture valuable exposure for their corporation.

Mastering the Art of Q & A is the first work to address systematically, comprehensively, and practically each of the risks listed above plus many others. The main ideas this book stresses are the importance of building credibility and maximizing control. From these concepts, described with numerous examples from my career as an executive communication consultant, flow all my analysis and advice, including that reflected in the highly practical set of preparation plans found in Part V.

The role of quality questioning—another often undervalued skill—is also emphasized throughout this book. Here you will find practical advice regarding the components of a quality question, the relationship between quality listening and quality questioning, the use of questions to enhance decision-making, and ways to plan questioning.

If you find yourself or expect to find yourself in important situations where your questioning or your ability to respond well to questions can make a difference between success and failure, then *Mastering the Art of Q & A* will definitely help you. Moreover, it can be your reliable companion for many years to come.

May this book bring you the mastery of Q & A you seek and deserve!

Myles Martel

PART I

THE BASICS

This section provides the foundation for most of the concepts discussed in this book by examining closely what a question is, what it can accomplish, and how the process of Q & A influences human behavior. Accompanying these insights will be a wealth of practical advice for both questioner and respondent.

CHAPTER 1: ASSESSING THE VALUE OF QUALITY QUESTIONS

1. How do questions influence you?
2. What functions do questions serve?
3. What are the implications of asking open-ended vs. closed-ended questions?
4. How can questions influence the quality of your decision-making?
5. What are the main objectives of a Q & A session?

CHAPTER 2: PROBING THE QUESTIONER'S AND THE RESPONDENT'S MINDS

1. What major factors influence the questioner while conceiving and posing a question?
2. What major factors influence the respondent while listening to, conceiving, and responding to a question?

3. Why do people over-answer?
4. What listening pitfalls are especially common in Q & A situations and how can they be alleviated?
5. What is the role of body language in the Q & A process?
6. How can you improve your ability to ask questions?

CHAPTER 1

ASSESSING THE VALUE OF QUALITY QUESTIONS

My firm recently purchased a new fax machine. Before we decided on which machine would best meet our needs, we met with several salespersons who represented the more popular brands. Although most of them were well primed to highlight the more appealing features of their models, few of them keyed into our specific needs by asking us such basic questions as:

1. How often will you be using it?
2. Will you be using it mainly to send or to receive?
3. Do you care particularly if the reproduction is made in roll versus separate sheet form?
4. How important is reproduction speed?

The sales representatives who did ask us the more basic and probing questions were the ones who more readily won our confidence. They won it by communicating via questions the message that they would recommend a machine that matched our needs—not one with a superfluous set of "bells and whistles."

Think about the office equipment, car, boat, stereo, or appliance salesperson you last dealt with. Or think about your physician, financial adviser, lawyer, close colleague, or friend. How many of these people inspired or failed to inspire your confidence because of their questioning?

Think about your own ability as a questioner. As a professional and consumer, can you improve your ability to ask the "right" questions in the "right" manner? Think of a professional or personal decision or major purchase you made recently. What role did quality questioning have in that decision? Put another way, how often have you wanted to kick yourself because you didn't ask one crucial question, the one that might have reversed your decision? Would you have asked it if you had simply taken the time to prepare a list of questions rather than "winging-it"?

As we evaluate our questioning skills, we shouldn't downplay our limitations. Fallibility in this area can be costly and reach into the highest of places. For example, did the FBI *really* ask Donald Ginzberg whether or not he had smoked marijuana when they screened him in 1987 for the U.S. Supreme Court? During the 1972 presidential campaign, why didn't George McGovern learn in advance that Thomas Eagleton, his running mate, had suffered from severe bouts of depression?

People who rely heavily on asking quality questions undoubtedly appreciate the role they play. But what specifically do questions do? How do they affect human interaction? This chapter answers these questions.

THE DYNAMICS OF QUESTIONS

Understanding the dynamics of questions can be valuable in planning any kind of meeting or transaction—from the simple purchase of a pen ("Does this have a fine tip?") to more pressing questions ("How should we reinforce our defenses against a potential hostile takeover?").

This list, which catalogues the major purposes for which questions can be used, can serve as a practical tool in preparing to ask and answer questions:

The Most Common Uses of Questions

1. *To discern/discover a basic fact:*
   "How late are you open tonight?"
2. *To discern/discover a causal relationship:*
   "Was programmed trading really a major reason for the stock market crash on October 19, 1987?"

3. *To promote searching inquiry:*
   "What is the true mission of this organization?"
4. *To introduce a policy discussion:*
   "Should we close our plant in Maine?"
5. *To solicit a position or opinion:*
   "Is the plant ready for a health and safety inspection?"
6. *To present an argument:*
   "How can a private club retain its claim to privacy while allowing 10,000 members to join it?" (paraphrasing an argument before the U.S. Supreme Court)?
7. *To challenge or reprimand* (and place the burden of response on the accused):
   "Why didn't you complete this assignment on time?"
8. *To accuse:*
   "Was it you coming in at 11:30, two hours after your curfew, or was it the Ghost of Christmas?"
9. *To seek direction:*
   "After I schedule these seminars, what should I do next?"
10. *To coax/suggest without being too directive or autocratic:*
    "Why don't we make sure the manuscript is in top shape before we start practicing the speech?"
11. *To probe a feeling:*
    "Are you finding this typing assignment wearing?"
12. *To demonstrate interest in another person:*
    "Did you enjoy the concert last night?"
13. *To demonstrate compassion:*
    "Being stuck in traffic for that length of time must have been incredibly frustrating?"
14. *To clarify a concept:*
    "What do you mean by 'shifting the burden of proof' when a hostile questioner tries to put you on the spot?"
15. *To request feedback:*
    "How was my follow-through on that swing?"
16. *To request support:*
    "Will you help me?"
17. *To request evidence/proof:*
    "How do you know for sure that someone in this

organization is leaking crucial information to the competition?"

18. *To probe a value judgment:*
"You referred to Rockwood as an excellent speaker. What do you mean by excellent?"

19. *To signal understanding of a problematic situation* (my wife to our housekeeper, frustrated that Ben, our golden retriever, was tracking large amounts of mud into our house):

Wife: "Do you have any suggestions? (without expecting an answer)
Housekeeper: "How about boots?"
Result: Ben now wears boots.

Each type of question identified above has one thing in common—it automatically makes communication two-way instead of one way. In many situations this factor alone increases the potential for understanding, quality decision-making, acceptance, outward support, improved morale, positive human relationships, productivity, and profits.

The "Smart Questions" Approach

Dorothy Leeds, a prominent management consultant, regards questions as so important that she has built an overall approach to management around them called "Smart Questions." Commenting on the value of questions, she states:

The main reason questions are so effective is that most people love to answer them. Questions stimulate the mind and offer people the opportunity to use their brains constructively.[1]

Of the numerous practical purposes that questions can serve in business, three highlighted by Leeds deserve particular

---

[1] D. Leeds, *Smart Questions, A New Strategy For Successful Managers* (New York: McGraw-Hill, 1987), p 23.

attention: motivating employees, taking the sting out of questions, and overcoming objections.

Motivating Employees

SITUATION   An employee comes to you with a suggestion regarding how to alleviate the parking problem around your office building.

RESPONSE OPTIONS   Your first reaction could be: "That sounds too expensive!" However, suppressing your opinion, you take the questioning route instead: "How much will it cost?"

ANALYSIS   By asking the question, you're allowing the employee to make his case before you pass judgment—to discover the flaws in his own case without your judgmental intervention.

Taking the Sting Out of Criticism

SITUATION   You have just instituted a system in which inquiries for your services are to be recorded on an inquiry form. For some reason, one of your employees fails to use it. As a result, he has not gathered several crucial pieces of information from the prospective client.

RESPONSE OPTIONS   You might approach him by saying: "Because you didn't use the form, we don't even know how to proceed with the inquiry." Or, you might prefer the questioning route: "Why didn't you use the inquiry form for that call?"

ANALYSIS   Not only does the question take the sting out of criticism, it provides the "accused" with the opportunity for a possible defense. For example, "The call came as I was closing up the office and the forms were locked away in my desk."

Overcoming Objections

SITUATION Your corporation depends on three computer operations centers spread across the country. As CEO, you've decided to consolidate them into one center near your headquarters. Colleagues and the employees in general fear that the change will result in reduced efficiency and eliminate the sense of security the multiple sites offer during major computer breakdowns.

RESPONSE OPTIONS You consider giving a speech detailing your faith in the consolidated operations center. However, on further reflection, you realize that this approach risks engendering counterarguments and hostility.

You decide instead to discern the specific concerns of your colleagues and employees through more private interactions and then hold a Q & A session.

ANALYSIS The Q & A session, although hardly risk-free, promotes the impression that you are interested and willing to listen. More important, it enhances your ability to respond to their objections.

Management consultant Eugene Raudseff has developed another classification scheme for questions. Among the more interesting types of questions he presents are:

The Off-the-Hook Question
This question allows the employee to refuse a request without feeling too awkward: "We've got this huge backlog of orders. I don't suppose you would want to help us by working a few extra hours tonight?"

The Invitation-to-Comply Question
This question involves an order softened by an "OK" appended at the end: "I know it will involve a lot of work, but we have to complete the job by this evening, OK?"

The Kill-the-Idea Question

Intentional or not, this type of question can limit any further idea development: "We should try this approach instead, don't you agree?"

"ZOOMING IN AND OUT"

The broadest method for classifying a question is by labeling it as open-ended or closed-ended. The open-ended question provides the respondent with a wide range of freedom in deciding how much to elaborate. The closed-ended question normally restricts freedom and, therefore, calls for a briefer response. The questioner's challenge, then, involves, deciding whether his purpose will be better served by a closed-ended question ("zooming in") or by an open-ended one ("zooming out").

Take for example the question, "Why did you make the switch from teaching to business?" This question, phrased in such an open-ended manner, could be attacked by tracing chronologically or topically the events that influenced the decision, while also containing essays about the worlds of education and business. If, however, the question were rephrased as "What was the single most influential reason you switched from teaching to business?" it would be more closed-ended. Still more closed-ended would be the yes/no question "Did you switch mainly because business represented an even better fit for your talents?" (However, even if the question is closed-ended, don't be surprised if it gets treated as open-ended.)

To clarify further, consider these questions: "If you could invite anyone you wish to dinner—anyone at all in the whole world—who would you select?" (a closed-ended question), "Why?" (an open-ended question), and "What types of questions would you be most interested in asking him or her, open or closed-ended? (a closed-ended question)."

To develop the skill of knowing when and how to "zoom in and out," let's consider the tactical implications of the open-ended and closed-ended question:

The Open-Ended Question

1. Facilitates overt involvement or the feeling of involvement.
2. May not be time-efficient.
3. Produces opportunities for follow-up questions.
4. Allows the respondent greater opportunity to control the agenda, even to the point of being nonresponsive.
5. Provides insights into the respondent's reasoning, intelligence, emotions, competence, and character.

The Closed-Ended Question

1. Reduces the need for further discussion. The closed-ended question, therefore, limits the potential for a high-quality, two-way flow of communication, although in many instances (e.g. accident investigations, courtroom appearances) a two-way flow may be unnecessary or inappropriate.
2. Is time efficient, providing time for additional questioning.
3. Can normally sound pointed and, therefore, can place the respondent on the defensive.
4. Helps maintain the questioner's sense of control, preventing the respondent's "agenda" from dominating the interaction.
5. Can efficiently test consensus or agreement: "Do we all agree that we should now focus on the open-ended question?"

QUALITY QUESTIONS AND SOUND DECISION MAKING

I'm sure we have all faced decision-making situations so filled with confusion, anxiety, or sheer frustration that we hardly knew where or how to begin. In fact, this state can become so pronounced that it can lead to decisional paralysis, a protracted delay that often allows the original condition requiring attention to worsen, for example, a leaky roof, an irresponsible child, an inefficient employee, or a weak marketing or advertising program.

One way to help yourself avert decisional paralysis is to embrace "issues analysis." This approach was introduced to me 30 years ago as a high-school debater. Since then it has proved helpful in my personal and professional decision-making.

Issues analysis involves a disciplined process of discovering the key questions that must be addressed before deciding on a contemplated action or change (called a "question of policy").

Questions of policy can be personal or professional. For example:

"Should I increase my son's allowance?"

"Should I buy a new suit?"

"Should we invite the Keefes over for dinner next Saturday?"

"Should our company replace all its electronic typewriters with word processors?"

Or they can be related to public policy:

"Should cigarette advertising be banned in the print media?"

"Should our township build a teen center?"

Any of these questions can generate several additional questions. Take for example the questions that can be generated by the question of policy, "Should we change our advertising agency?"

1. Are their advertisements working for us?
    a. How can we evaluate their impact?
    b. How much of the impact is related to:
        (1) The design of the ad?
        (2) The market for which it is targeted?
        (3) The media chosen?
        (4) The timing of the radio and television buy?
        (5) The frequency of the ad's appearance in various media?

2. Is our business experiencing changes that make our agency less qualified to meet our needs?
3. Are we satisfied with the agency's attention to our ongoing needs?
4. Do they give us a good range of choices?
5. Do they adequately change their approaches as we provide feedback?
6. Do they meet our deadlines?
7. Has the agency experienced personnel or clientele changes that undermine their ability to meet our needs?
8. Are their fees in line?

This simple example highlights the advisability of identifying (possibly through brainstorming) those potential issues requiring discussion. The next step is to reduce your list of potential issues to those crucial issues or questions that *must* be answered to resolve a question of policy.

Let us turn to a more complex issue. Suppose you are a United States Senator discussing with your advisors the question of policy: Should the United States offer birth control counseling and devices to nations that request them? To enhance the quality of your deliberations, you collectively produce the following list of questions or issues:

1. Do the economies of these nations suffer because of the absence of population control?
2. Can current food production meet the demand of the population today and 10, 20, or 30 years from now?
3. Do world conditions necessitate controlling the population explosion?
4. Would a program of providing birth control counseling and disseminating birth control devices be successful?
5. Does the high birth rate decrease the per capita income and savings of these nations?
6. Does the population explosion increase the threat of war?
7. Could religious groups, for example, the Catholic Church, quash this proposal?
8. Is such a program financially feasible?
9. Is such a program consistent with the ethical, moral and religious values of the people of the United States?

Which of the nine questions above qualify as key questions—questions crucial to making a responsible decision regarding the question of policy? Only four: 3, 4, (8,) and 9.[2]

The remaining questions are important, however. They ask questions about the issues themselves, not about the main question of policy. Once answered, these "important" questions help you determine the validity of any position taken on the issues. For example, examining the capacity of food production to meet future population needs would be significant in answering crucial question 3: "Do world conditions necessitate controlling the population explosion?" But a "yes" or "no" response to the food production issue does not automatically commit one to providing or denying birth control counseling and devices as an answer to the basic question of policy.

STOCK ISSUES: THE NEXT STEP

Once you have differentiated between the crucial questions, the important questions, the less important, and the irrelevant, you can benefit from developing a structure in which these questions can be addressed. A stock-issues approach helps provide that structure.

Stock issues are standard questions that provide a framework for decision-making as well as help you discover additional crucial or important questions. They apply to questions of policy, fact, and value.

Stock Issues for Questions of Policy

Stock issues for questions of policy fall into four categories: need, plan or solution, feasibility, and advantage. Each category will be highlighted in the context of the question of policy, "Should we move our offices to a new building?"

---

[2] Number 8 is in parentheses because some would argue that the merits of questions of policy should be addressed before examining considerations of cost.

1. *Stock Issue of Need*
   "Is there a need or compelling reason for a change?"
   Specific Issues
   a. "Does our present building meet our anticipated need to expand?"
   b. "Is the building conveniently located for employees and our clients?"
   c. "Is it properly maintained?"
   d. "Does the building make a statement congruent with our firm's image?"
2. *Stock Issue of Plan or Solution*
   "Can the need be met?"
   Specific Issue
   "Is office space that meets our needs available?"
3. *Stock Issue of Feasibility*
   "Can the policy resolve the need or problem without inviting 'new' headaches?"
   Specific Issues
   a. "Can we afford the basic moving expenses?"
   b. "Can we afford the new space?"
   c. "Can we make the move with minimal business interruption?"
   d. "Can we afford the redecorating expenses?"
4. *Stock Issue of Advantage*
   "Will extra benefits accrue from the plan?"
   Specific Issues
   a. "Will the new building have a better security system?"
   b. "Will it have a cafeteria?"
   c. "Will it have a health and fitness center?"
   d. "Will it provide a better base for potential clients than our current building?"

Causal Analysis and Plan Criteria Issues

Causal analysis and plan criteria issues complement the capacity of the stock issues to promote quality decision-making. Causal analysis issues probe the reasons why something has happened or is happening. Plan criteria issues create a basic framework for assessing the "fitness" of a plan or solution:

Causal Analysis Issues

1. "If a problem or compelling need for a change exists, why? For example, why isn't the current building being well maintained?"
   a. "Is building management weak?"
   b. "Do they have a poor relationship with the maintenance firm?"
   c. "Has management lost interest?"
2. "Are any one of these possible reasons an actual cause or a coincidence?"
3. "If a cause, is it the only cause?"
4. "How significant is this cause?"
5. "If there are other causes, how significant are they in creating the need or problem?"
6. "Are the collective causes so significant that they require a major change (e.g., a move) versus another approach (e.g., hiring your own maintenance firm)?"

Plan Criteria Issues

1. What criteria should apply to selecting the best possible plan or solution? (e.g., location, attractiveness, expansion potential, quality of maintenance)
2. What resources are most important? (e.g., affordability, time, etc.)

Stock Issues for Questions of Fact and Value

The specific questions generated by the stock issues and the causal analysis and plan criteria issues are either questions of fact or questions of value. To ensure quality decision-making, these questions can often benefit from a stock-issues approach.

Stock Issues for Questions of Fact

"Will it have a better security system?" is one example of a question of fact that could benefit from a stock-issues approach. In this instance, the stock issues serve as general questions that help one to discover the validity of a premise or claim.

Stock Issue:

"On what basis can I validate the claim?"

Specific Issues:

1. "Will building management provide reliable information regarding the security history of the building and area?"
2. "Can the policy be helpful?"
3. "Should we retain a security consultant?"

The rigor of a quality legal encounter, particularly one involving a dramatic incident or emotional issue, provides further understanding of the value of stock issues in answering questions of fact. In these encounters, the issues focus on whether or not the statement of fact is valid and properly classified. The issues of validity deal principally with what we as witnesses observe directly or indirectly. The issues of classification involve inferences or conclusions based on what we observed.

To clarify your understanding, consider this example: Miniver Cheevy is shot to death by Richard Cory. In assessing the validity of this statement of fact, the following stock issues involving direct or indirect observation surface:

- "Was a body discovered?"
- "Do we know for sure that it was Miniver's?"
- "Is there a report from a qualified person that the body contained a gunshot wound?"
- "Did the medical examiner conclude that the gunshot wound was the cause of death?"
- "Do eyewitnesses to the shooting exist?"

On the more inferential level, three separate stock issues surface:

1. "Did Mr. Cory shoot Mr. Cheevy intentionally?"
2. "Did he do it upon reflection or deliberation?"
3. "Was the act justifiable?"

Stock issues also apply to other types of legal actions, for example, perjury:

1. "Were legal charges pending?"

2. "Was the accused a witness?"
3. "Was he under oath?"
4. "Did he knowingly testify falsely?"

For any of the sets of questions provided above, the defense attorney needs to provide only one negative answer to a single stock issue for the defendant to be found not guilty. The questions have in effect become the criteria for classifying the crime and the verdict.

Stock Issues for Questions of Value

"Is this a *good* report?" is a question of value with the dominant issue term being "good." How do we appraise the "goodness" of the report? Through questions like, "What criteria can be applied to such an assessment?" and "On what basis can we assess the conformance of the criteria with the object or idea being described?"

Considering the issue at hand, you may wish to identify the practicality and the readability of the report as your definition of "good" and, therefore, as the principal criteria for assessing the "goodness" of the report.

Q & A SESSIONS: OBJECTIVES AND OPPORTUNITIES

The value of a Q & A session depends on your opportunity to meet one or more of four principal objectives:

1. To clearly communicate and reinforce your key messages.
2. To assess your audience's levels of understanding and agreement.
3. To diffuse criticism.
4. To convey to your audience that you value their input.

As a general principle, a Q & A session should not follow a message intended to stand by itself, for example, a keynote address, certain after-dinner speeches, ceremonial addresses such as commencements, award presentations, dedications, retirement and anniversary speeches, and, of course, eulogies.

A significant and potentially controversial internal announcement before a large assembly of employees may not be appropriate for an immediate Q & A session. However, smaller breakout Q & A sessions scheduled soon after may be advisable. In fact, I have seen this approach work extremely well in announcing new products and promotions, mergers, reorganization plans, layoffs, and plant closings.

CHAPTER 2

PROBING THE QUESTIONER'S AND THE RESPONDENT'S MINDS

When millions of Americans were riveted to their TV sets during the summer of 1987 to watch Colonel Oliver North and others testify on the "arms for hostages" deal, their attention was captured by a compelling drama. This drama was accentuated by the significance of the issues being raised, by the cloak-and-dagger intrigue, and by the importance of the personalities involved, especially their closeness to the President.

One other factor contributed to this drama—the dynamic tension between questioner and witness, a battle of wits and words the American people hadn't seen since the Watergate hearings 14 years earlier.

This chapter provides insight into the dynamic tension between questioner and respondent by probing what goes on in their minds. In addition, it offers advice regarding the most important mental activity affecting both—listening—and presents programs for enhancing the quality of both listening and questioning.

INSIDE THE QUESTIONER'S MIND

As a mediator and arbitrator for 20 years, I have resolved a wide range of cases, including scores of unique disputes that fall outside the realm of labor relations. For example, I mediated a turf-related dispute among balloon salesmen at the Philadelphia Zoo, another involving movers who dropped a piano down a flight of stairs, and several cases dealing with seemingly irreconcilable differences between family members working in the same business. Crucial to my effectiveness in this role was my ability to listen and to ask questions. And since I had to concentrate intensely on both at the same time, the challenge was formidable.

But no less formidable are the pressures facing a lawyer taking a deposition or trying a case, a reporter conducting an interview following a crisis, an executive reacting to an important presentation, a detective interrogating a witness to a major crime, or an employer interviewing a person for a key position. And no less formidable are the pressures facing the respondents in each of these situations.

As we examine these pressures, it is important to note that we will be discussing a "process." The Q & A interaction is not a simple step-by-step process in which first a question is asked and then an answer is provided. Real-life Q & A involves a myriad of thought patterns and behaviors simultaneously initiated by both questioner and respondent.

Understanding this process first requires focusing on the questioner's goals. Sometimes the goals are carefully thought out; at other times, the questioner has thought little about them. Whatever the case, the questioner should decide specifically what he or she wants to accomplish? "Truth" is certainly an appropriate general goal for most, if not all, situations, but it is not specific enough to help us develop lines of questioning and to stay focused on what they are supposed to achieve.

The Process in Perspective

To illustrate this point, let's say that you are the COO of an organization seeking its first head of communications. You want the candidate to be a good manager with a solid background in internal publications, in dealing with the media, and in your field. You've prepared your lines of questioning based on these criteria and are focused squarely on one goal: determining whether or not each candidate interviewed is the "right match" for the position.

A prime candidate has just entered your office for an interview. In approaching this or almost any type of interview, realize that your role as interviewer involves a dimension of control—or even power—in the interaction between you and the interviewee. Thus, when the interviewee questions you, the control or power balance shifts.

During this or any other Q & A exchange, you, as questioner, should be primarily interested in three major components of the interaction discussed below: The quality of your questions, the quality of your performance, and the quality of respondent's overall performance.

The Quality of the Questions

As you are formulating or asking a question (e.g., "What do you find satisfying and less-than-satisfying about your current position?"), several thoughts may occur to you regarding it.

> "What is the specific objective of this question in relation to my goal? Is it designed to acquire information, to make a point, to challenge the interviewee in some manner, or to accomplish some other objective?"
>
> "Is this question appropriate (vs., for instance, too personal)?"
>
> "Am I phrasing this question clearly?"
>
> "Is the question as penetrating as it should be?"
>
> "Is the question difficult for the respondent to avoid answering?"
>
> "How much information should I reveal in the question; for example, could I bias the response by revealing my bias? Might I disclose something important in making my case (a lawyer's concern) or in solving the case (the detective's concern)?"

The Questioner's Interest in His Performance

Once you have phrased the question, your attention should turn to how it is worked into your line of questioning and to considerations regarding your overall performance:

1. "Is this the appropriate time to ask the question? Is it too early? Does more rapport need to be built first?"
2. "Should I ask more than one question at a time to make sure that my questions get asked?" (a major concern for reporters at a heavily attended news conference)
3. "How aggressive must I act to get recognized, or in asking follow-up questions?" (another major concern to reporters)
4. "What image or tone should I project? Cordial? Warm? Distant?"
5. "How good a listener should I be *and* appear to be?"
6. "How will my body language support or detract from that image? How should I sit or stand? Should I smoke?"

Focusing on your image goals question 4 is particularly important because your tone or image will not only influence your ability to secure helpful answers, but, especially in a job interview, will affect the interviewee's assessment of his compatibility with you. Questions 5 and 6, regarding listening and body language, will be discussed later in this chapter.

The Questioner's Interest in the Respondent's Performance

As you are asking questions, you need to be just as focused on the respondent's performance. Specifically, you should ask yourself the following questions:

1. "Is he answering my questions? If not, why? Does this reflect an inability to understand the question? Evasiveness? A tendency not to focus well?"
2. "How clear are the answers? Is clarity or lack of clarity potentially significant to the position? For example, does it reflect a lack of intelligence or possibly an inability to communicate that might impair his performance?"
3. "Are his answers reasonably to the point or more rambling? If he meanders, is this a negative sign, for example, a lack of mental discipline or respect for time?"
4. "What is the intrinsic quality of the substance of the responses?"

5. "What traits does the substance transmit? Competence? Flexibility? Insight? Intelligence? How confident can I be in making these inferences?"
6. "What traits are transmitted by body language (both vocal and visual)? Interest in the position? Security? Patience? Sincerity? Respect?"
7. "Does the respondent initiate questions or is he or she mainly reactive? If mainly reactive, is this a negative or a positive sign?

Mental and Environmental Noise

Despite the questioner's intense focus on the interview, other factors can create "mental or physical noise" that can impede or occasionally facilitate the process. For the executive conducting an interview, it might be a preoccupation with a personal or business issue, or getting to the next meeting on time. For the reporter it might be concern about meeting a deadline, "scooping" the competition, or, as with the executive, making the next appointment. In addition, either the executive or reporter, or both, could be distracted by "external noise" such as ringing telephones, loud voices, shutting doors, sirens, and beepers.

The Mind of the Respondent

The respondent, while seeking to accomplish specific goals, is just as prone to being inundated by the same type of pressure-inducing concerns.

1. "Did I hear the question correctly?"
2. "Do I understand it? If not, should I ask that it be repeated or rephrased?"
3. "Can I answer it? If not, what do I say?"
4. "Why is the questioner asking this question?"
   a. "Should I ask him?"
   b. "What are the risks (personal, political, or legal) surrounding a response to this question?
   c. Am I walking into a trap with a reporter, lawyer, or detective—or a challenging business situation?"

5. "How responsive should I be?"
6. "How long or detailed should my response be?"
7. "To what extent should I dissect the phrasing and assumptions of the question as part of my response?"
8. "To what extent does this question provide me with an opportunity to advance my persuasive goals?"

The Respondent's Self-Interest in Overall Performance

In addition to focusing on the response itself, the respondent needs to be aware of his or her overall performance. The following questions place these concerns in perspective:

1. "What image do I want to emphasize? Competence? (for job interviews and most other situations); compassion? (in responding to a crisis situation involving a health hazard, death, or injury); strength? (in seeking a major leadership position)."
2. "To what extent should I initiate questions? How?"
3. "What positive, nonverbal cues should I transmit? What negative ones should I avoid?"
4. "What listening behaviors should I be attuned to?"

The Respondent's Interest in the Questioner's Performance

The respondent actively makes inferences regarding the questioner's performance, including such questions as

1. "Are the 'right' questions being asked?" "If not, why?"
2. "What inferences can I make, based on verbal and nonverbal cues, regarding interest in me (a job interview), understanding of the information or issue (most any situation), or the slant of a story (reporter). How confident can I be in these inferences?"
3. "What inferences, based on verbal and nonverbal cues, can I make regarding the resoucefulness, personality, and character of the questioner? Intelligent? Friendly? Honest? How confident can I be regarding these inferences?"

WHY DO PEOPLE OVERANSWER?

Recently I met with a sales executive who was bursting with energy and enthusiasm, fed in part by great confidence in his products. Although he was as delightful a person as you could ever meet, he had one serious problem: When I asked him a question, I could have gone to lunch and returned while he was still answering that same question.

Clearly, one of the major dangers a respondent faces in any type of interview is overanswering a question. Although the communication, image, and tactical implications of overanswering will be discussed in detail in Chapter 6, it is appropriate to review why people overanswer.

1. One reason is that the difficulty of the question requires processing time. The respondent launches into a stalling explanation to buy time for the answer he really wants to give—and frequently fails to produce it.
2. The respondent may be uncomfortable with silence and would rather keep on talking than experience the discomfort—however brief.
3. The intellectual depth of the question could stimulate an ego-fed reaction within the respondent that the answer must equal or surpass the question's depth—despite the fact that "yes" or "no" might be a perfectly adequate answer.
4. The respondent may possess a general lack of confidence reflected in a need to overanswer—a need driven by a conscious or subconscious sense that doing so will produce an enhanced sense of control and possible acceptance.
5. The respondent may be concerned that too brief an answer may appear curt or terse and therefore overcompensates by overanswering.
6. The respondent may lack confidence that the answer is sufficiently understood or believed (although the audience's feedback may have been misread) and engages in unnecessary repetition and detail.

7. The respondent may have an inflated sense of how interesting or entertaining he is.
8. The respondent may be unjustifiably defensive and, as a result, defend or justify positions or actions with over-elaborate explanations.

Defensive overanswering can frequently result in what persuasion theorists call the "boomerang effect." As you are trying to persuade your audience, your overanswering raises additional doubts about your cause instead of convincing your audience of its merits. As Shakespeare said, "Me thinks the maid doth protest too much."

LISTENING WITH THE EAR AND EYE

Do you remember Gerald Ford's gaffe in his 1976 debate with Jimmy Carter when he repeatedly stated that there was no Soviet domination over Eastern Europe? If you do, you probably remember asking yourself and others, "Why did he say that?" Although a precise answer is elusive, if not impossible, poor listening was definitely a factor. I have repeatedly analyzed a videotape of the debate and have drawn three specific conclusions. These conclusions highlight how poor listening resulted in a gaffe that many political observers claim helped prevent Ford's return to the White House: (1) Ford's level of *emotional intensity* in delivering his response to the original question was so strong that he was too focused on speaking and not on listening. (2) As a result, he *interrupted* Max Frankel, the questioner, as he was asking his follow-up question. (3) In so doing Ford failed to listen with his eyes and ears to the *verbal, tonal, and visual cues* that he had misspoken.

We're all guilty of these listening sins, but to prevent ourselves from committing them in high stakes/high risk situations, we should be familiar with what quality listening is and what we can do to become more effective at it.

In the questioner-respondent relationship, quality listening plays several key roles. Beyond promoting comprehension, it allows the questioner to decide whether or not to ask follow-up questions, which ones to ask, and how much to persist. For the respondent, quality listening promotes understanding the question, provides the option of dissecting its assumptions (stated or implied), increases sensitivity regarding the questioner's intent, and facilitates recall (especially if the question is long or complex).

The Components of Listening

Listening is a four-step process involving hearing, attending, understanding, and remembering.

Hearing
Hearing should not be confused with listening. Hearing is a physiological process in which the sensory receptors of the ear are stimulated by sound waves. A voice that is too soft can first make it difficult to hear—and then to listen. Conversely, loud background noise can have the same effect.

Attending
Our attention faces competition from a wide range of stimuli surrounding us. As you ask me a question, my phone rings. Although I attempt to pay attention to you, my mind wanders to "I wonder who's calling." I forget your question and ask you to repeat it. I feel embarrassed. You may or may not feel offended.

To be an effective listener—and a good questioner and respondent—you must be focused, tuning out distractions such as people walking out of the auditorium, crying babies, beepers going off, television cameras and lights going on and off, motorized cameras clicking in your face, microphones being placed less than 2 inches from your Adam's Apple, etc. In fact, shunning these distractions can actually be a sign of sophistication.

Understanding
This step involves decoding the stimuli we have heard and attended to into a message that makes sense. For this to occur, we must have a shared language-base reinforced by clarity (Chapter 5). If I ask you whether or not you have ever experi-

enced the "boomerang effect," you would have heard, attended to, and understood my question. However, before reading this chapter, you may have never heard of the "boomerang effect." Therefore, you would not have understood me because we did not share a language-base.

Remembering

This represents the process of storing what we heard, attended to, and understood. Memories are like fingerprints: no two are exactly alike; we all retain and forget various types of information differently. However, in a legal or quasijudicial setting (e.g., an arbitration or a legislative hearing), a weak memory can be the basis for inpugning your credibility, one of the opposing attorney's major goals during cross-examination.

Fixing Bad Habits

Of the many types of listening pitfalls, four are especially common in the Q & A setting.

Feigned Listening

Feigned listening is when we make believe we are paying attention by maintaining eye contact, nodding our heads, saying "I see," and providing other nonverbal and verbal cues to indicate listening. This pitfall can be especially pronounced when the respondent is so prepared to respond that he acts attentive to the questioner while saying to himself, "Hurry up and finish so I can answer."

Sporadic Listening

Sporadic listening is often used with feigned listening. It involves a tuning-in-and-out process in which your understanding of what was said is based on piecing together what you did listen to, however poorly or well. To an extent, Gerald Ford's listening before he committed his infamous gaffe was sporadic.

How many times have you been conversing with someone when a radio or TV message catches your ear and your interest? Basic politeness prevents you from saying that the distraction is more important than your conversation. Therefore, you sporadically listen both to the person you're conversing with and to the distraction.

In the Q & A exchange, sporadic listening affects both questioner and respondent. As a questioner, it is common to listen sporadically because you are thinking about your next question or line of questioning as the respondent is presenting an answer. As a respondent, you face a similar risk. While being asked a question, you may be engaging in sporadic listening as you rethink the answer you just gave and rush ahead to respond to the question you *think* is being asked.

Argumentative Listening
This pitfall, sometimes called "verbal battle," involves preparing a counterargument as you listen to a question or answer. As you do, you may be missing the full spirit of what was asked.

Inefficient Notetaking
Recently I was interviewed by a reporter whose distracting habit of taking copious notes made me wonder whether or not he was missing my main ideas while he appeared to be catching words or phrases as if taking intermittent verbatim dictation.

Anyone who relies on a notepad rather than a tape recorder should ask three questions: (1) "To what extent might you be missing the main points because you're trying to capture a quote:," (2) "To what extent might you miss a quote because you're doing a lot of notetaking to capture the main point?," and (3) "To what extent do you frustrate the respondent—and curb his spontaneity—by influencing his pacing by the style and speed of your notetaking?"

In contrast, efficient notetaking via key words can be a most helpful listening aid. Moreover, it can demonstrate interest in the respondent's remarks.

Active Listening

No better method exists for ensuring effective listening and comprehension than active listening. Active listening involves making sure you understand what another person is saying by restating your understanding of their message. The person then provides feedback regarding whether or not you understood sufficiently, and clarifies the point(s) you did not understand. You then have the option of "feeding back" your understanding of the clarification. In a Q & A exchange between a feature reporter and an executive communication consultant, active listening might work like this:

REPORTER

What does an executive communication consultant do?

CONSULTANT (as Active Listener):

Do you mean specifically what projects we work on or how we address them?

REPORTER:

What projects you work on.

CONSULTANT:

We prepare people for speeches, presentations, and media appearances.

REPORTER (as Active Listener):

You mean you write speeches and coach people to deliver them?

CONSULTANT:

We mainly edit speeches, advise people how to deliver them, and prepare them to face the media.

REPORTER (as Active Listener):

So you don't necessarily write the speeches?

CONSULTANT:

Correct. Often our role in addition to coaching is strategic and editorial.

REPORTER (as Active Listener):

Strategic. What does that mean?

CONSULTANT:

Analyzing the audience, shaping the ideas, and phrasing and organizing the message to achieve a certain objective.

REPORTER (ending the active listening process):

Oh, I see.

Active listening can be especially effective in informal meetings, cross-examination, and print interviews. However, it's use in larger forums and before the electronic media is more limited because neither environment supports the extended exchanges that active listening often produces.

BODY LANGUAGE IN LISTENING

Listening with your eyes is just as important as listening with your ears. As you are questioning someone, or as you are being questioned, which of these cues common to Q & A are present?

Interrupting questioner:	Impatience, defensiveness, aggressiveness, lack of respect for questioner or audience.
Looking down or away:	Possible sign of timidity, insecurity, dislike, difficulty with the question, the need for "private" thinking time.
Smiling:	Confidence, embarrassment ("you got me"), pleasure (that question was asked).
Scratching head:	Discomfort, the need for thinking time, and yes, a simple itch.
Turning body away from audience:	Discomfort, defensiveness, the need for "private" thinking time.
Walking toward audience:	Confidence, a desire to engage or create a more personal or intimate feeling.

Folding arms across chest:	Defensive or unable to find an appropriate relaxed position.
Tilting head and chin upward:	Confidence, arrogance.
Nodding head:	"I understand," "I agree," "Hurry up and finish."
Shaking head:	"I don't follow you;" "I disagree."
Holding chin before responding:	Reflection, sometimes indicating difficulty with the question.

The context will help you interpret these body language cues and others. And remember, if a cue is particularly pronounced and you are having difficulty interpreting it, you may want to ask a question about it, for example, "Why are you shaking your head?" If you don't, you may be limiting your potential as a quality listener.

"SURVIVAL" GUIDELINES FOR QUALITY LISTENING

As you commit yourself to capitalizing on your potential as a listener, consider the following advice:

1. Be mentally and physically prepared to listen with your eyes and ears; make the commitment!
2. Think about the topic in advance if possible.
3. Avoid interrupting the speaker.
4. Take brief "key word" notes.
5. Use active listening to make sure quality communication is taking place.
6. Demonstrate to the speaker your interest and alertness.
7. Provide clear and unambiguous feedback.
8. Withhold evaluation of the message until the speaker is

finished and you feel you understand both the overall intent and the key facts and assumptions of the question or response.

"SURVIVAL" GUIDELINES FOR QUALITY QUESTIONING

1. Decide specifically what goals and objectives you want to accomplish.
2. Prepare in advance questions keyed to each of your objectives. (Don't overlook the value of relying on the timeless list: who, what, why, when, where, and how.)
3. Define what image or tone you should project. Do you want to put the respondent on the defensive? Make him lose composure? Or encourage a sense of trust and confidence in you?
4. Be aware of how your nonverbal or body-language cues support or undermine your goals. Do you nod understanding? Smirk to project disagreement? Turn away to indicate disinterest? Question too aggressively as in cross-examination?
5. Be sure that the language and the phrasing of your question is clear.
6. Consider beginning with easier and less-threatening questions and then moving to more challenging ones.
7. If you are not satisfied with a response, ask a follow-up question rather than succumb to impatience or a false sense of understanding.
8. Pay close attention to the respondent's body language. What messages does it suggest? Do any of the body language cues contradict the stated message?
9. Pay close attention to your own listening ability— including your notetaking style and its impact on your listening.
10. Provide enough time for the person to respond.
11. Be fully prepared to be questioned yourself.

PART 2

IN CONTROL

When, during the 1980 Presidential Debate, Ronald Reagan took the stage and caught Jimmy Carter by surprise by walking over to him to shake his hand, he was not merely being polite, he was sending a powerful message to 120 million viewers—that he was in control.

No single concept discussed in this book is more important than control. This includes control of yourself, your credibility, the environment—the audience, setting, format, and timing—as well as control over your message—the ideas, the source, and the words.

As you read this section you will be introduced to the 11 Commandments of Q & A that support control: credibility, character, candor, competence, confidence, composure, concern/compassion, cooperation, compatibility, clarity, and conciseness.

In short, this section helps you to take stock of how much of your management talent is being applied to managing your Q & A sessions and provides a practical framework for preparing for any Q & A exchange.

CHAPTER 3: CONTROLLING YOUR
CREDIBILITY AND SHAPING YOUR IMAGE

1. What are the components of credibility and its role in the Q & A exchange?
2. How can credibility be enhanced?
3. What is the role of confidence in Q & A and how is it conveyed?
4. What factors influence loss of composure and how can composure be maintained?
5. What is the role of concern or compassion in Q & A and how can it be communicated?
6. What is the role of image in Q & A?

CHAPTER 4: CONTROLLING
YOUR Q & A ENVIRONMENT

Controlling the Audience

1. What is audience analysis and how can it help you in a Q & A exchange?
2. What is targeting and how can it be useful to you?
3. How can you describe the relative intensity of your audience's attitudes?
4. How can you conduct an audience analysis?

Controlling the Setting

1. How does the setting influence a Q & A exchange?
2. What major questions should you ask in selecting a suitable setting?

Controlling the Format

1. How can format influence a Q & A exchange?
2. What specific points should you keep in mind in designing or approving a format?

Controlling the Timing of Your Message

1. Why is timing important?
2. How can it affect audience interest?
3. How can it affect news coverage?
4. How can it affect attendance?

CHAPTER 5: CONTROLLING YOUR MESSAGE

1. What are net effects and substance goals and how do you set them?
2. How does controlling the source influence controlling the message?
3. What major factors should influence the phrasing of your question or response?

CHAPTER 3

CONTROLLING YOUR CREDIBILITY AND SHAPING YOUR IMAGE

No single factor in the dynamic relationship between the source of a message and its receiver or audience is more significant than credibility. No matter how clear, insightful, sensitive, or eloquent a message may be, if it is not credible, its potential impact will be compromised.

Whenever you are making a speech or presentation or fielding questions, you are possibly activating one or more of five channels of credibility:

1. Your own personal credibility
2. The credibility of your ideas
3. The credibility of your corporation
4. The credibility of your division, department, or company within the corporation
5. The credibility of your business, profession, or industry.

If you were an executive of a large pharmaceutical company asked to defend the safety and effectiveness of one of your highly controversial cardiovascular products on a national television talk show, you should do everything possible to cultivate at least three channels of credibility:

1. *Your own personal credibility.*
   Are you a physician? Are you a cardiologist? Do you have family care experience? How familiar are you with the research behind your product? How prepared are you to

defend the fact that the pharmaceutical firm issues you a weekly paycheck?

2. *The credibility of your ideas (the safety and efficacy of the product).*
   How much confidence can we derive from the research? How legitimate are the complaints? How widespread are they? What is the Food and Drug Administration's reaction to the complaints?

3. *The credibility of your corporation.*
   What is your corporation's record in dealing with controversial products? Does the public or do the media regard your past conduct as responsible? If the product is regarded as one of the pillars of your corporate success, how would you respond to accusations that your motives are more profit-oriented than consumer-oriented?

The two remaining credibility channels might also be activated in a situation like this: the credibility of your division within the corporation (pharmaceuticals) and the credibility of your industry as a whole, for example, "Are big drug firms prematurely marketing unsafe and ineffective products?"

The effective persuader is the advocate who understands which channels of credibility need to be cultivated and to what extent. The effective persuader is also the advocate who knows how to leverage his credibility to make a less than palatable point or proposal more acceptable.

MAJOR COMPONENTS OF CREDIBILITY

Eight traits, all drawn from the 11 Commandments, constitute the principal components of credibility: character, candor, competence, confidence, composure, concern/compassion, cooperation, and compatibility.

Character

Character is the keystone of credibility. If we feel that the speaker's character is flawed, particularly our perception of his truthfulness, then our ears are likely to deafen to even the most inspired thinking. Witness the catastrophic loss of trust experienced by Gary Hart, Jim Bakker, Joe Biden, and Jimmy Swaggert, four of America's dominant political and religious personalities whose transgressions of character either destroyed or severely weakened their following.

Character, particularly trustworthiness, can be more obvious by its absence than by its presence. Normally, we accept a person's word unless we have reason to feel otherwise. If we do feel otherwise, we sense that the person's motives may seriously conflict with ours. This helps explain why we may feel skeptical when buying a used car, real estate, etc.

Although character can be conveyed through references to one's religious activity and teachings, we should be careful not to parlay it too explicitly. Doing so could promote the impression of self-righteousness ("wearing it on your sleeve") or the inference that we are compensating for a hidden character flaw.

Prior reputation, not self-proclamation, is therefore the best means to convey character. If this reputation is not known by the audience before an engagement, then the introducer can cover it in a manner that prevents the speaker from being perceived as egotistical or self-righteous.

Candor

When I think about how time promotes historical perspective I turn to Harry S Truman, a man whose presidency overflowed with controversy. Yet today Truman ranks among the most admired Presidents, in part because of his ability to make the tough decisions (dropping the A-Bomb, initiating the Berlin airlift, recognizing Israel, firing MacArthur) and partially because of a quality relevant to this section—candor. Harry Truman epitomized the plain-spoken man from Missouri. His style in conversation and in public speaking was direct, crisp, unadorned and, in fact, candid to the point of brutal.

REPORTER:

Mr. President, I see that among the candidates for the Nobel Peace Prize are President Peron of Argentina and my colleague Mr. Drew Pearson. Were either of them nominated by the government of the United States?

TRUMAN:

I can say categorically that they were not. Probably nominated themselves.

Candor may indeed bruise feelings, but its potential to promote credibility is enormous, for the candid person expresses himself in a manner seemingly oblivious to hidden meaning and hidden agendas.

Candor is an especially desirable quality for spokespersons and for most anyone who faces tough questioning. The candid spokesperson or CEO in a crisis situation, ambush interview, or televised public hearing is prone to give the impression of truthfulness; he does not appear to be masking the truth in a sea of well-honed phrases that "reek of the company line."

Competence

As we assess a person's credibility, the factor that normally influences us the most is our perception of his or her competence. Competence implies that experience or study has given this person a vantage point for making statements worthy of our trust.

Appraising competence can be complicated. Take, for example, a contested presidential primary in which a wide field of contenders woos the voters' support. Some of the candidates may be members of Congress, some former cabinet members, one or more a current or former vice president or governor. As we review their varied candidacies, we establish conscious or subconscious subjective criteria to make a decision based largely on competence: leadership experience and results, grasp of the issues, proposed programs, and vision.

During a Q & A session, competence can be communicated in three principal ways: by the perceived insightfulness of a response, by the instant grasp of facts or points on which to build a response, and by references to experiences, accomplishments, or results that the audience values or admires.

Many persons I advise have difficulty folding references to their accomplishments into their responses. Some do not mainly because of personal style; others are concerned that such references may sound too immodest or self-serving. However, if one's natural style is reasonably down-to-earth or nonegotistical, the likelihood of sounding conceited or self-serving is usually remote.

Generally the greatest resource for intentionally conveying competence is by referring to travel, meetings with important people, books or articles read or written, research, personal association with significant events, media appearances, speaking engagements, and seminars attended (e.g., Harvard's Advanced Management Program). In fact, skillfully handling such references can help elevate your perceived level of competence to one of expertise.

Confidence

My clients tell me that they generally feel more confident during the Q & A exchange than during a speech or presentation. There are four reasons for this: (1) a question implies audience interest or relevance, something the speaker often feels uneasy about during his formal remarks; (2) the Q & A tends to be more personal or one-on-one than the presentation, prompting a more comfortable, conversational style—one that contrasts with the need to sustain verbalization imposed by more formal remarks; (3) questions, however challenging or benign, tend to get our competitive juices flowing, normally resulting in a more comfortable and expressive style; and (4) the Q & A forum has an important ego-gratification component—it allows you to display your expertise.

Although the Q & A session may often be conducive to confidence and greater comfort, it has its obvious risks: the risk of making a misstatement, the risk of having your theory or basic premise dissected or decimated, and the risk of not knowing the answer to a question your target audience feels you should know.

Each of these risks can be reduced significantly through well-planned practice and feedback sessions. My own experience confirms this: I have prepared CEOs for scores of demanding shareholder meetings and political candidates for well over a hundred debates and can count on only one hand the total number of important "surprise" questions posed.

The Confident Image and the 3 "V's"

A confident image inspires our confidence in what the respondent has to say. In fact, if we don't sense a confident image, the person's credibility may actually be at risk. The confident image has three interdependent dimensions, which I call the three "Vs": verbal, vocal and visual.

The Verbal Dimension. What factors contribute to a confident verbal image in responding to questions?

1. Sounding decisive at the beginning of the response as opposed to "wimpy," wishy-washy, or meandering.
2. Having little difficulty producing the appropriate word or expression.
3. Not pausing too long before responding. (However, a brief thoughtful pause is often advisable.)
4. Avoiding inelegant fillers or vocalized pauses such as "um," "er," "you know," and "like."
5. Displaying conviction—a sense of personal identification and commitment—in expressing ideas.
6. Avoiding unnecessary qualifiers (sometimes called "authority robbers") such as "I think," "I feel," "I believe." For example, which of the following works best if you're the CEO answering a question posed at your annual sales meeting. "What kind of year do you think we're going to have?"
   a. "I think this should be a terrific year for us."
   Or,
   b. "This should be a terrific year for us."
7. Infusing the phrasing with energy produced by sentences of short and medium in length vs. ponderously long sentences (a friend of mine calls them "anacondas") and by words that connote power or activity. Note the big difference that changing only one word makes in the semantic strength of the following two sentences:
   "Our sales growth last year was strong."
   "Our sales growth last year was explosive."

The Vocal Dimension. The vocal dimension has five major components: articulation, rate, emphasis, projection (volume), and pitch.

Articulation refers to our capacity to enunciate clearly versus embodying the opposite extreme, mumbling, a speech pattern that not only undermines our ability to understand, but also our sense of the speaker's authority and conviction.

Rate or speed *of speech* has fascinating implications for perceived confidence. We normally speak between 140 to 160 words per minute. If we speak too slowly, we might be perceived as not confident, dim-witted, or both. If we speak quickly, we could be perceived as confident, verbally facile, or, to a more opposite extreme, nervous.

Emphasis, including the amount of energy you inject into a word or phrase, helps to communicate your level of conviction or commitment, an important dimension of your confidence and overall credibility. This conviction, properly expressed, can give contagious energy to your ideas, thus enhancing their believability. For example, John F. Kennedy, in his first debate with Richard Nixon in 1960, delivered an 8-minute opening address at an average of 220 words per minute, almost 40 percent faster than our normal speaking rate. Was he talking too fast? Absolutely not. His emphasis patterns, accentuated by repetition and pausing, contributed to an arresting cadence, and helped produce a supremely confident vocal image.

Volume or projection helps promote the speaker's confidence and conviction. As soon as the Q & A session begins, you should *project* your invitation for questions in a confident voice: "And now I'll be pleased to answer your questions." This approach outdistances the diffident and qualified, "I'll try to answer your questions if you have any."

Pitch involves how vocal sounds fall along a musical scale. When we say that a speaker is monotonous, we are referring to a flat pitch level, regardless of whether the sounds produced are spine-chillingly high or as low as the bass in a jazz combo.

Confident vocal expression requires the ability to vary pitch to communicate our range of emotions more fully and stimulate our audience's attention and interest. Moreover, broadening your range of pitch can result in a greatly enhanced sense of self-expression.

The Visual Dimension.   Our eyes play a large role in evaluating a person's confidence, especially since so many visual cues are related to presence:

Attire and grooming.   Neat grooming and attire imply self-respect. Poor grooming or untidy or wrinkled attire may imply an even stronger negative message.[3]

Posture and position.   Slouching over the lectern as a human dust cover might make you more relaxed and feel more engaging, but an erect posture behind the lectern or, when possible, in front of it can transmit a powerful message of openness and confidence.

Eye contact.   Fair or unfair, the world is filled with people who regard lack of eye contact as a sure sign of lack of confidence. Worse yet, many people regard it as a sign of deceit. Eye contact is important for three principal reasons: it projects confidence, thereby promoting credibility; it makes communication more personal; and it allows you to read the questioner's or the target audience's feedback, thereby allowing you to adjust your answer if they haven't heard you or are disinterested, bored, don't understand or disagree with you.

The smile.   Many of the executives I have advised have had difficulty smiling while making speeches and presentations and fielding questions. I attribute this to three basic causes: a tendency to be more focused on the risks the engagement represents than on the opportunity—including the opportunity for enjoyment—it offers; a fear that smiling could transmit a negative message, for example, that he is not taking the message or the audience seriously enough; and a lack of understanding that an appropriate smile can not only convey confidence, but also can project a sense of friendliness leading to trust and approachability.

Usually the executive begins to smile after I encourage him to relax his facial muscles, to visualize a more positive relationship with his audience, and to value the credibility implications of a genuine smile. Success is even greater if my observations

---

[3] This book will not provide advice regarding attire, especially since styles change so often. However, refer to the bibliography for a few helpful references.

are reinforced by a videotape replay of a stoic, dour—or sour—visage.

Gestures.   Most people I advise have little difficulty gesturing during a Q & A session (although they may have difficulty gesturing during the presentation itself). Gestures are important; they convey confidence and conviction and can significantly complement your emphasis patterns.

When appearing on TV, avoid far-reaching gestures; instead, keep your hands close to your body and away from your face.

Placing one hand in your pocket while gesturing with the other is normally appropriate, although it may be too casual for more formal settings.

Distractions.   Recently I advised a trim, mature, impressive-looking executive how to field questions. His listening behavior was excellent, his posture was appropriate, his answers were informed, responsive, and to the point. Only one thing was wrong. During his responses he played with his keys and pocket change, behavior picked up and amplified by his microphone.

Not only was this a distraction, it was also a confidence robber. Other distractions capable of undermining our perception of a presenter's confidence are playing with notes or a paper clip, taking too many sips of water, crossing one's chest (defensively), walking away from the audience (reflectively or defensively), scratching one's head, playing with one's mustache, being easily distracted. The list goes on. However, if these behaviors are brought to the presenter's attention, they usually can be controlled.

Composure

Few of us will forget the contradictory image projected by Alexander Haig, Jr., Secretary of State, on March 30, 1981, the day Reagan was shot, when he said forcefully, while shaking and perspiring heavily, "I am in control [of the White House] here. . . ." And few Philadelphians who followed the energy crisis in the early 1970s will forget the oil executive who, when accused by the media of being a party to manipulating the crisis, blew his cool on live TV with "That's the dumbest f———g question I ever heard."

If a Hall of Shame were erected for all the bright, talented people who dramatically lost their composure in a demanding Q & A exchange, we would need to build a skyscraper. And while it is easy to criticize or ridicule someone for losing composure, we must understand the factors that can lead to loss of composure.

Loss of composure is generally brought on by a highly tense state in which a question or comment is the "straw that broke the camel's back," by an assault—real or perceived—to one's ego, or by both. This condition is often exacerbated by a sudden sense of lost control manifested as frustration—frustration that you don't know what to say in response or how to say it.

Composure Detractors

Consider the following specific factors that can lead to loss of composure during a media interview, annual meeting, public hearing, debate, or other encounter:

- The accumulative tone of the questioning challenges your credibility—and assaults your ego.
- You are confused as to the amount of force you want to display in response, for example, should you question or attack the questioner?
- The questioning is getting repetitious, implying a lack of belief in what you are saying.
- The aggressiveness of the questioning and/or the restrictiveness of the format is preventing you from having enough time to think and to present your key messages.
- The questioner has disclosed a surprising piece of disturbing information you wish you had learned earlier.
- As you're responding to the questions, you're rethinking a previous response, deciding whether or not you wish to retract or to build on it.
- You don't know an answer to a question that you and the audience realize you should know the answer to. As a result, you feel embarrassed, or worse, humiliated.

- The hot television lights, the TV cameras, and other distractions are making you even more uncomfortable.
- Beads of perspiration are starting to appear on your face and you worry about their impact on your credibility and on your overall image.

Although the chapter on Managing Hostility (Chapter 9) will provide more in-depth advice regarding composure vis-a-vis hostility, two pieces of advice seem especially appropriate here:

"If you're angry, count to five.
If you're really angry, count to ten."

Thomas Jefferson

Do your best to keep your ego out of the picture—to depersonalize the situation—while responding to the issues at hand. Yes, this is a tall task, but you really don't have a choice—other than the Hall of Shame.

Concern/Compassion

As the CEO of the Coast of Maine Clam Chowder Company (CMCCC) you learn that one of your larger shipments of chowder is contaminated, resulting in approximately 70 people suffering from food poisoning, five of whom are listed in critical condition. With little hesitation you recall the entire shipment, although media pressure is mounting for you to recall every can of chowder you've produced. Your sense of disappointment and frustration defies description: a full recall could seriously weaken the financial stability of CMCCC if not put it out of business. Yes, you feel sorry for the victims, but your emotions are focused more on the many years you've devoted to building the business, on your employees, and particularly on the business risks you are facing.

Your spokesperson has convinced you that you should call a news conference to update the media on CMCCC's intentions. How should you proceed?

Step One is obviously to put aside any illusions that your main position should be to focus on the economic risks of the full recall. Step Two is to define a consumer-oriented approach to the entire crisis, beginning with an opening statement which should emphasize these points: You are very sorry about the misfortune facing the victims and their families. You have a reputation for being a responsible company that has long manufactured a quality product. Your customers have been crucial to your good reputation and success. And your actions have the customer's interests—particularly their health and safety—uppermost in mind.

By projecting concern and compassion, you have now set the tone for a news conference that should help cultivate your corporate credibility.

Credibility, concern, and compassion: how are they related? Concern and compassion, properly expressed, strengthen your trustworthiness, and thus your credibility. If you are genuinely concerned about me, I am more likely to find you trustworthy and, therefore, more credible.

How often do you find that concern or compassion missing when you expect it the most?:

CAR OWNER:

"This is the third time in the last six weeks I've brought my car to you to fix the same problem. I'm a salesman and I need the car for my livelihood. How can I be sure it will be fixed right this time?"

INSENSITIVE SERVICE MANAGER:

"What can I say?"

SENSITIVE SERVICE MANAGER:

"I'm sorry you're having these problems, Mr. Childs. I will personally see that this problem is addressed by our most experienced mechanic, and do everything I can to make sure that it will be fixed right this time."

In many Q & A situations, the questioner may be more interested in your expression of concern toward him than in your answer. The question, therefore, may be merely a vehicle to solicit your reassurance, empathy, or support.

COMMUTER TO TRANSIT OFFICIAL:

I'm late for work three out of five days a week. Why can't the trains run on time?

ANALYSIS The commuter may not want an explanation of why trains don't run on time. In fact, the commuter probably knows that equipment failure is the main reason. What he really wants from his comment/question is an opportunity to vent his frustration and to judge or solicit the Transit Official's concern.

TRANSIT OFFICIAL:

I'm sorry that you've been late for work. Getting people to work on time is extremely important to us and we're doing everything we can to improve our on-time performance. (*Optional*) For instance, we've purchased 35 new cars and constructed a modern maintenance facility, which should reduce equipment failure and make it more likely that your train will be on time.

Cooperation

Cooperation is an important component of credibility, especially in media relations. Reporters expect company spokespersons to be respectful of their deadlines and responsive to their requests for interviews, background information, and research.

By being cooperative, the spokesperson is conveying two implicit messages: first, that he and his company have nothing to hide; second, that he values a positive working relationship with the media.

Being cooperative also has a credibility-preserving function related to control. Consider this scenario: A reporter requests information that you are reluctant to provide because it will probably embarrass your company. However, you realize that the reporter could secure the same information from a source outside the company. Should you cooperate? Probably, especially since not cooperating might injure your relationship with the reporter, possibly causing the company to be even more embarrassed by the manner in which the information will be used.

Compatibility

Compatibility, projected mainly by sociability or likability, is an important component of credibility, especially if you are deciding whether or not to include the person on your team or are choosing someone, for example, a customer service representative, who needs to be compatible with others. It can also influence your comfort level in asking a person a question and can thereby relate to approachability.

What main factors, then, promote our liking of another person? Psychologist Eliot Aronson in his study, *The Social Animal,* concludes that we achieve compatibility with people whose attitudes and interests are similar to ours; those who offer genuine praise and perform "no-strings-attached" favors; those who have special talents or competencies and such qualities as loyalty, kindness, and reasonableness; and, of course, those who like us in return.[4]

In encounters in which the speaker is not known well by his audience, compatibility is conveyed mainly via five factors: a general sense of friendliness; common ground references to shared perceptions, values, and experiences; good humor; a sense of direct contact with the audience; and a general sense of comfort and self-assurance without the impression that he is taking himself too seriously.

CULTIVATING YOUR CREDIBILITY

A good measure of your credibility will be generated naturally. However, in the spirit of control, it is wise to ask yourself if you are doing your utmost to project credibility during your Q & A session or media interview. These specific questions should prove helpful.

- Without being too self-serving or egotistical, are you prepared to fold into your responses credentials that qualify you to speak on the topic?
- Do you use examples enough in your responses— especially examples that can impress the audience with your breadth of experience and success?
- Do you take sufficient advantage of common ground opportunities to highlight in a genuine way similarities in

---

[4] Eliot Aronson, *The Social Animal* (San Francisco: W.H. Freeman, 1980), pp. 237–270.

attitudes, feelings, and experiences between you and your audience?

- Do you project the impression that you have done your homework for the audience you are addressing—an impression that gives them the feeling that you have made a special investment on their behalf?
- Do you take pains to make sure the audience appreciates the personal value of your point of view and senses your genuine interest in them?
- Do you project the proper image of respect and liking for the audience? Do you smile easily? Can you display humor to promote a sense of "oneness" with them?
- Do your responses have a sufficient ring of authority and conviction?

SETTING YOUR IMAGE GOALS

Although credibility and any number of its principal components should dominate a person's image of you, other more specific image considerations may come into play. Take for example George Bush's need to counter his "wimp" image during the 1988 presidential race. Specifically, he was perceived by large segments of the media and the public as a weak, nice guy who lacked the courage of his convictions—or even any convictions at all.

To offset this image, his advisors encouraged him to sound more forceful, forthright, and even contentious. This latter advice resulted in his highly publicized combative exchange with the *Des Moines Register's* Jim Gannon, moderator of the debate before the Iowa caucuses, and with CBS's Dan Rather during a personal interview a few weeks later.

You, too, should take an inventory of not only what credibility commandments you need to convey, but also what specific image traits you need to project regarding yourself or any of the credibility channels you represent. Do you need to project strength, decisiveness, patience, or some other trait? Do you need to promote the impression that your corporation, division, industry, or profession is aggressive, action-oriented, and tough, or that it embodies some other trait(s)?

I call this inventory process "setting your image goals." This exercise, which complements the process of setting your message or substance goals (Chapter 5), should be conducted as you determine as specifically as possible how your target audience perceives you. Politicians use polls to establish image goals, while executives generally rely on less formal means of feedback (although more formal systems can be devised). The table below should prove helpful in setting your image goals:

Image Traits

Indicate adjacent to each item the number from the scale below that represents the frequency with which the following traits are projected. If you feel that the trait—or its apparent opposite—is particularly dominant, circle the appropriate term.

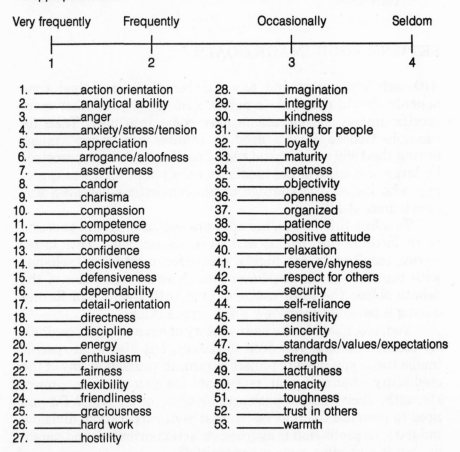

Very frequently	Frequently	Occasionally	Seldom
1	2	3	4

1. _____action orientation
2. _____analytical ability
3. _____anger
4. _____anxiety/stress/tension
5. _____appreciation
6. _____arrogance/aloofness
7. _____assertiveness
8. _____candor
9. _____charisma
10. _____compassion
11. _____competence
12. _____composure
13. _____confidence
14. _____decisiveness
15. _____defensiveness
16. _____dependability
17. _____detail-orientation
18. _____directness
19. _____discipline
20. _____energy
21. _____enthusiasm
22. _____fairness
23. _____flexibility
24. _____friendliness
25. _____graciousness
26. _____hard work
27. _____hostility

28. _____imagination
29. _____integrity
30. _____kindness
31. _____liking for people
32. _____loyalty
33. _____maturity
34. _____neatness
35. _____objectivity
36. _____openness
37. _____organized
38. _____patience
39. _____positive attitude
40. _____relaxation
41. _____reserve/shyness
42. _____respect for others
43. _____security
44. _____self-reliance
45. _____sensitivity
46. _____sincerity
47. _____standards/values/expectations
48. _____strength
49. _____tactfulness
50. _____tenacity
51. _____toughness
52. _____trust in others
53. _____warmth

CHAPTER 4

CONTROLLING YOUR Q & A
ENVIRONMENT

The President of the United States has a team of advance men who visit a city or town weeks before his appearance. Their role: to determine the public's reaction to his upcoming visit, to do everything feasible to reduce the element of surprise, and to make sure that the setting, format, and timing of his message place him in the most advantageous light.

Even if you do not have an advance man, you or someone designated by you (preferably your communications officer) should do everything possible to understand your audience—whether your presentation is in-house or external—and to determine your latitude for controlling the setting, the format, as well as the timing of your message. This chapter provides practical advice for achieving these forms of control.

KNOW THY AUDIENCE

Few of us will forget the three weeks of highly contested U.S. Supreme Court confirmation hearings in 1987 over the ill-fated nomination of Judge Robert Bork. During his 32 hours of testimony, Bork was asked by a friendly senator the most predictable question of all: "Why do you want to be on the Court?" Instead of presenting a patriotic essay about the honor and privilege of preserving freedom and the Constitution, Bork said that serving on the court would be "an intellectual feast."

This answer was one of several that reinforced Bork's image

as a cold-blooded ideologue. In fact, even a key supporter implied that he had not tailored his answers to his audience and the setting: "This was a political event, it was not a trial or a law school debate."[5]

No message can reach its potential impact unless it is tailored to the needs, wants, desires, values, or goals of an audience. The speaker who is too self-centered or too content-centered is normally doomed to mediocrity—or to failure. Enter audience analysis.

Audience analysis is used to learn as much as possible in advance about your audience before you speak and before you field questions. This process applies to any type of engagement within or outside the organizaton.

Audience analysis has three principal components: demographic analysis, knowledge-level analysis, and attitudinal analysis. This scenario places the practical nature of audience analysis in perspective:

> As a leading manufacturer of contractor pumps you are invited to address a plumbing and heating contractors' convention session regarding "Hydro-Thrust," an innovative pump your firm has just manufactured. Before you prepare your remarks, you decide to secure answers to the following questions, classified according to the three components of audience analysis.

Demographic Analysis
How many people are expected to attend?
How many will be plumbing versus heating contractors?
How many will be dealers?
How many will be your customers?
Will there be others?
How many are already using the "Hydro-Thrust" pump?

---

[5] Al Kamen, "The Bork Crusade Against 'Radicals and Leftists,'" *The Washington Post*, March 27, 1988, p A8.

Knowledge Level

How familiar are they with the basic design of a contractor pump?

To what extent do they have the technical background to understand the "Hydro-Thrust" design?

How familiar are they with the featured advantages of the "Hydro-Thrust" design over conventional pumps?

Attitudinal Analysis

How satisfied or dissatisfied are they with the pumps they currently sell or use? Why?

How do they feel about the "Hydro-Thrust" pump? Why?

How do they regard your company? You? Why?

MAKING YOUR AUDIENCE ANALYSIS WORK FOR YOU

Let's assume the following conclusions from the "Hydro-Thrust" audience analysis described above: You decide that your primary target audience is characterized by dealerships that sell to major contractors, and also includes the major contractors themselves. You learn that their experience with and understanding of the "Hydro-Thrust" pump is minimal, and although they respect your company, they know little about you. You also learn that their attachment to the leading competitive product is moderate to extremely strong, mainly because of reliability and price.

These few facts should promote the following tactical approaches to both the presentation and the Q & A: Since the audience is not familiar with you, you will need to find ways to cultivate your credibility and overall image (Chapter 3); and because your target audience's knowledge level of "Hydro-Thrust" is minimal, you will need to educate as you persuade. As you do, choose language, concepts, and examples suited to the interest, experience, and level of understanding of your target audience. Explain the advantages of "Hydro-Thrust" with fair-minded comparative references to the leading competitive product. Persuading your audience to substitute a new criterion associated with "Hydro-Thrust," (e.g. faster water evacuation) for reliability or price is apt to be challenging. However, if "Hydro-Thrust's" reliability is strong and the price issue is nonexistent or modest, then the water evacuation capacity feature, if appreciably greater than the competitive product's, may offset concerns regarding price. If that's the case, then you should highlight "Hydro-Thrust's" reliability, competitive price, and water evacuation feature early in the presentation, while underscoring the economic benefits of faster evacuation.

The basic lesson this example provides is that your audience analysis is crucial to both your presentation and Q & A as you select ideas, language, and examples, and shape a pattern of organization. To paraphrase the American Express ad, "Audience analysis is a must; don't leave home without it."

AUDIENCE ANALYSIS, TARGETING, AND THE INTERNAL PRESENTATION

Audience analysis tends to be underutilized in internal situations. Although executives rely on general sources of input regarding their audience or committee, such as whether they are for or against a particular proposal, they seldom take their analysis to the next step—to determine the specific reasons *why.*

"Why" information is crucial to knowing how to preempt arguments within the presentation itself and to build on them during the Q & A. If we don't understand the "why's," we weaken the links between the benefits of our proposal and the audience's needs. We therefore shun the essence of persuasion.

During your internal committee meetings, who are the key people you need to "sign on" to get your proposal moving? The CEO? CFO? Chief counsel? Head of Human Resources? How do their positions—their frames of reference—influence the types of questions they ask? More specifically, *where* do they stand regarding your proposal? *Why?* How intensely?

Intensity can best be described according to the following scale:

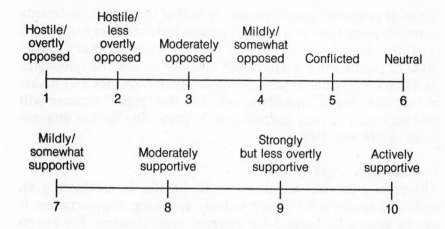

As you interpret the data gathered from your audience analysis, you can normally rely on two widely recognized principles of persuasion: The greater the hostility or support, the less the susceptibility to persuasion, especially conversion. Therefore, one's persuasive energies should generally be concentrated primarily on people with opinions in the 4 to 7 range on the scale, unless the principal persuasive goal is reinforcement.

You may be asking, "What if my target audience members fall below the 4 range?" In such instances, you should not rely too heavily on the presentation and the Q & A session to produce the support you seek. Rather, you may need to develop a campaign built on internal lobbying and multiple presentations in which you persuade your audience to "buy into" your proposal on an incremental, issue-by-issue basis.

Obtaining Information about Your Audience

Four principal methods are available to you in conducting a quality audience analysis: the telephone interview, private meetings, informal contacts, and the formal survey.

The Telephone
If you have an outside speaking engagement or plan to be making a presentation before a prospective or current client, picking up the telephone to ask one or more reliable sources a

series of prepared questions can be one of the best investments in preparation time you make. In some instances, for example, a speaking engagement, you can prepare your secretary, assistant, or public information staff member to ask the questions. And don't worry about the impression such inquiries will make; in fact, the "right" questions asked in the "right" manner will probably convey your earnestness in preparing for the engagement or presentation.

Private Meetings
Although a private meeting can be helpful in conducting an audience analysis for major outside speaking engagements, it can be especially helpful for internal presentations. For example, if you are planning to make a major presentation and expect resistance from key audience members, meeting with them in advance cannot only help you discern where they stand and why. Moreover, it can also provide an opening for your persuasive advances.

Informal Contacts
Valuable audience analysis information can be obtained deliberately or occur spontaneously in the most informal settings—over coffee, lunch, in the hallway, or on the way to work. The company grapevine can provide the latest information regarding who is or is not attending your presentation and what the current "pulse" is regarding it. However, before you accept any of this information as gospel, do your best to verify it. If you can't, and the information is crucial to your message, decide in advance how you should adjust your message just in case the "grapevine" proves itself reliable.

The Formal Survey
The formal survey may seem a bit unorthodox, but I have used it most successfully for several of my own speaking engagements. I draft the survey, the host organization distributes it and returns it to me for tabulation and interpretation. I then base my remarks on it, often referring specifically to the data during both my speech and the Q & A session.

The main advantages this approach provides are specificity

and accuracy. Rather than merely relying on the input of a few members of the host organization, you can secure data from most, if not all, of the audience.

CONTROLLING THE SETTING

A client of mine, the president of a highly respected laboratory, was invited to appear on national television as an expert on medical testing. As we prepared for the interview, we explored how we could "control" the visual image—the setting in which the interview would take place. One possibility was inside the laboratory. However, the laboratory, while impressively large and clean, had few pieces of equipment to reinforce strongly one of his key messages: technical sophistication. Another possibility was to stand at the entrance to the building, under the name of the laboratory, but this would not be too impressive either, especially in inclement weather. The third possibility, the executive's office, was finally selected because it was at least a comfortable setting for him. This visual image was to be buttressed by supplying the network with aerial views of the laboratory plus videotapes from the sister laboratory on the West Coast, where more sophisticated equipment is housed. We therefore took control of the setting.

How much latitude for controlling the setting do you have in planning for important meetings and media appearances.[6] To clarify this, you might ask if the room is large enough? Are the lighting and electrical conditions appropriate? Are the facility and room conveniently accessible? Do you have ample opportunity to use visual aids? Are furnishings congruent with the personal image you intend to project? Is the room decorated in a manner that supports your key message or theme? Is the seating ample and comfortable? Do seating arrangements allow you to be seen easily?

---

[6] The preparation plans (Section V) clarify further your range of control.

CONTROLLING THE FORMAT

The format you select for a Q & A session can not only influence how a message is received, but can actually convey its own messages. The following example puts this point in perspective:

> Recently I prepared the executives of a large manufacturing firm to make a full-day presentation to their board of directors. The program had three purposes: to better familiarize the board with the business, to give them confidence that the firm's strategy was on target, and to showcase their management team.
>
> During the planning stages, the president stated that he didn't want the board to feel that the program was a one-way "propaganda campaign" or "snow job." He therefore decided to reserve lengthy Q & A periods following each major presentation, expecting the announced length of the Q & A sessions to communicate the management team's openness and confidence.
>
> This format increased the probability of risk—the risk of a member of the management team making a misstatement, generating unhealthy disagreement between management and the board, or not knowing the answer to a question. However, despite these risks, the team drew confidence from the president's assurance that they could perform well within the more open format.

Another example representing a keen understanding of the importance of controlling the format involves the management of a large membership organization I represent. They decided to propose to their membership a plan to restructure the organization significantly. The plan had been carefully thought out, but the concrete need for it was difficult to sell because it was based on future assumptions and hard-to-quantify arguments.

Part of the organization's strategy to secure membership approval was to "presell" the plan in a series of meetings with key members. To do so, the plan's advocates took two major tactical steps: first, to diminish the possible perception of too hard a sell, their "presell" meetings were focused not only on the plan, but also on other issues of concern to members; second, several of the meetings were restricted to groups of 6 to 8. This prevented an opponent from making a persuasive statement that might have otherwise influenced a larger group of members.

Other issues of format control that might affect you include whether you want to appear on a panel or show with an adversary. Ask youself whether the appearance will do more to neutralize his impact or elevate his legitimacy.

Also, during a Q & A session, do you want to answer questions until people stop raising their hands, or do you want to end the session (possibly with the help of a program chairman) on an appropriate upbeat note (see Chapter 8)? If you are on a panel, what speaking position do you prefer? Or does appearing on the panel (versus being a featured speaker) diminish your status? Are certain topics off limits to your audience for legal, personal, security, or proprietary/competitive reasons, or because of a lack of sufficient expertise? If so, be prepared to maintain control by saying so— and be prepared to hold the line.

CONTROLLING THE FORMAT IN MEDIA INTERVIEWS

Controlling the format, as this example highlights, also applies to media interviews. A few months ago I received a call from the spokesman of a public official I serve. The official had been accused by the media in headline stories of "junketeering"— using taxpayers dollars for unnecessary foreign travel. The situation had become so intolerant that the official decided to put a halt to media interviews. That is until a well-recognized reporter requested one more, claiming that he hadn't had an opportunity for an exclusive on the issue. The reporter promised the official one more opportunity to tell his side of the story. We agreed to the interview, but stipulated that it be confined to the official's travel and not be focused on other controversial issues with which he had been linked. We also requested that the reporter, in explaining the official's terms of acceptance, not say that he "refused" to discuss the other issues; rather, the reporter should indicate that the interview was granted on the proviso that it focus only on the travel issue. We took control of the format, allowing the official to clarify his position.

CONTROLLING THE TIMING OF YOUR MESSAGE

The tireless axiom "timing is everything" may be at most only a slight exaggeration in its relevance to you as a communicator. That's because timing can significantly affect three important communication variables: the size and make-up of your audience; their level of active participation; and the overall impact of your message.

Political debates pose a good example of the importance of timing. The candidate who needs the additional exposure a debate affords would prefer that it occur on the most popular channel during prime time on the evening his target audience would most likely tune in. His opponent, if obligated to debate, would want the complete opposite (as a debate negotiator and advisor for many years, I should note that negotiations over such matters can reach a fevered pitch).

Imagine yourself as the CEO of a major food company planning to announce via a news conference a new, revolutionary, low-fat, low-cholesterol food product. Recognizing that timing is key to generating maximum coverage, you select a day when you don't expect a major competing story that will prevent the reporters from attending your news conference (e.g., the scheduled announcement of a verdict in a major case, Election Day, etc.). As well, you select a day when viewership and/or readership is normally strong and an hour when you can take full advantage of the day's—or the next day's—news cycle.

The influence of timing on the second variable, the audience's level of participation, can be especially significant if you seek a good amount of give-and-take between speaker and audience. For this reason, you develop a format conducive to two-way communication and sensitive to the audience's personal schedules and their fatigue factor. For example, I have seldom seen good Q & A sessions follow a weekday luncheon address that ends after 12:45. Reason: normally people are more interested in returning to work. Moreover, the meal may have created a physiological reaction which saps their energy and, therefore, their eagerness to participate.

In some instances your timing tactics may be focused on limiting two-way communication. For example, if you're the CEO of a publicly held company facing horrendous financial problems, you may want your annual meeting to be as short as possible without drawing attention to your intent. Therefore, if you have a choice of 10:00 or 10:30, you will probably opt for 10:30 since noon or close to it may be perceived by much of your audience as a sensible time to end (although you should not bank on such assumptions). In addition, you may decide to lengthen the various meeting addresses to limit exposure to potentially embarrassing audience questions.

The third variable related to timing, the overall impact of your message, is brought into focus by this scenario. You are planning a three-day national sales meeting with an address at some point from your chairman, a decidedly inspirational speaker. Where do you place him in the program? At or near the beginning to set the tone? Somewhere in the middle to help offset any drag in the program? At the end to send the sales troops home on a powerful note? Not an easy decision. However, by raising questions such as these you are reflecting your appreciation of the need to exercise control over timing.

CHAPTER 5

CONTROLLING YOUR MESSAGE

QUESTION:
Why does the President of the United States begin his press conferences with an opening statement?

ANSWER:
To control his message—to lay out the points he wants to emphasize and to preempt difficult questions that can be more easily answered during the opening statement.

This chapter will discuss the three principal aspects of controlling your message: controlling your ideas by setting goals; controlling the source; and controlling the words.

SETTING NET EFFECTS AND SUBSTANCE GOALS

The starting point to controlling your message is by setting your net effects goals—defining the specific attitudes, feelings, or behaviors you wish to result from your Q & A exchange. Net effects goals can be positive or preventive, overt or covert. For example, let's say that a reporter is interviewing you regarding price-fixing charges recently leveled at your company. During the interview some of your net effects goals would probably be: to convince the reporter—and ultimately the public—that the charges are groundless (positive/overt); to project the impression that your company has a reputation for fair-dealing (positive/overt), to prevent your own employees from questioning further your business practices (preventive/covert). To prevent the erosion of your customer base (preventive/covert).

The next step to controlling your message to set your substance goals—deciding what specific key points you wish to transmit to your target audience to help satisfy your net effects goal. As you do, it's important to realize that most of your messages are to some extent persuasive; that is, in varying degrees they seek to influence the audience's attitudes and/or behavior. When identifying your key messages, ask yourself how much background information the audience needs to understand your ideas? Are the key messages sufficiently distinct to prevent the perception of overlap? Are the messages selected and framed in a manner conducive to persuading or informing your target audience? Are they sufficiently limited in number to prevent confusion or dilution of your intended impact?

Careful preparation based on these questions provides a stronger foundation for responding to questions properly, for remember, *the Q & A session is usually a forum for actively advancing your key messages.*

As straightforward as the preceding questions may be, setting net effects and substance goals can be complicated, especially if multiple audiences need to be courted. For example, I recently advised the head of a national interest group that represents a somewhat controversial line of consumer products. As we analyzed his role as a communicator, it became clear that he had at least *three* different messages for *six* different audiences

1. The consumer, legislators, regulators, and the secular press: "The product line is safe."
2. The financial analysts: "The product line should enhance sales and profitability."
3. The trade association members: "The product line, if subjected to extensive government regulation due to issues of safety, could undermine the financial stability of member institutions."

Controlling a message can also involve not commenting.

QUESTION:
>   Why did I recently refuse to answer a reporter's specific questions regarding my services to a public agency now under media fire by saying "My work with my clients is confidential?"

TWO REASONS:
>   First, I did not want to give added life to a negative story affecting my client. Second, I wanted to reinforce my reputation for keeping confidences. By communicating very little while making my point, I controlled my message.

Over the years, I have attended many "Town Meetings" conducted by members of the U.S. House and Senate for their constituents. One I attended in Western Pennsylvania a few years ago was unforgettable. The most vocal attendees were unemployed steelworkers who showed up with their families— including their infants—to vent their protest and to plea with natural eloquence and compelling passion for the Federal government to do more to reverse their lot. The Member of Congress I accompanied undeservedly symbolized the insensitivity of the government and was subjected to a heavy dose of verbal abuse. However, throughout the session he maintained composure and projected genuine compassion; then he wrapped up the session with a few short remarks that emphasized his key messages. His performance, including his attempt to control his message at the end, was a portrait of appropriate, effective control.

CONTROLLING THE SOURCE

When planning a TV commercial, you can decide who your spokesperson should be, for example, a well-known personality, consumer, corporate executive (Lee Iacocca, Victor Kiam, Frank Perdue), an unknown actor, or some combination of the above. You can also decide how long they should appear, when, and, of course, what they say. These decisions are solely based on your assessment of the potential for persuasive impact.

Such assessments are becoming more scientific than subjective. Increasingly, corporations are relying on focus groups for input in identifying the best spokesperson not only for commercials but also for media appearances. Groups of eight to ten people meet to view videotapes and discuss the relative strengths and weaknesses of each spokesperson. In fact, one technique involves each focus group member turning a wheel that electronically registers reactions on a graph.

Whether the focus group or electronic device makes sense for you, your responsibility is to select the best spokesperson(s) available: men and women whose credibility meet the criteria discussed in Chapter 3 and whose communication skills and understanding of the issues are unmistakably strong.

Controlling the source has special pertinence in crisis situations. Consider this comparatively simple scenario: A public school bus carrying 43 students from public, private, and parochial schools slips on the ice and rolls over an embankment at 7:45 one wintry morning. Ten students are rushed to a hospital for treatment of lacerations and broken bones.

In this situation alone, the following persons could be pressed into service as de facto spokespersons: the bus driver, representatives from the school system providing the bus, representatives from the schools attended by the students, plus the students themselves, parents, and eyewitnesses. Hence the potential for a hugh chorus of discordant voices speaking before cameras, lights, and microphones regarding what happened and why. This simple situation explains why corporations have spokespersons and crisis plans. By controlling the source they can control the message.

CONTROLLING THE WORDS

The three principal criteria for controlling the phrasing of the message are clarity, conciseness, and the capacity for the message to generate and maintain the audience's attention.

Clarity

QUESTION TO A PH.D. IN COMMUNICATION:
    "What is clarity?"

ANSWER:

Essentially clarity is a phenomenon characterized by idiosyncratic selective perceptual behaviors that result in a conscious or subconscious state of recognition that a message or its constituent elements is relatively devoid of factors that tend to facilitate cognitive confusion in the receiver.

IMAGE MESSAGE Pretentious! Out-of-it!

CLARITY QUOTIENT (*without careful rereading*) Low

How ironic it is that this hypothetical Ph.D. in communication can't be clear in defining clarity. But that's the point. Clarity is a challenge facing all of us, regardless of intelligence, education, or position—or knowledge about communication.

Let me ask the question again: "What is clarity?" In simple terms clarity means that a message is understood with minimal confusion. What factors from the example above promote confusion and thereby undermine clarity?

- Answers or sentences that are too long or complex (example above: 42 words)
- Answers or sentences that contain too many concepts (example above: at least five)
- Answers containing jargon (example above: "selective perceptual behaviors," "cognitive confusion")
- Answers containing highfallutin language when simpler, more direct terms would be more effective: "idiosyncratic" = unusual/uncommon, "constituent elements" = components/parts, "devoid of" = free from, "facilitate" = promote, "cognitive" = mental
- Answers that are too abstract or not sufficiently concrete (example above in its entirety)

The absence of structure or direction to a response also undermines clarity:

QUESTION:

As an executive communication consultant preparing people for challenging situations, what would you consider to
be their major needs?

ANSWER 1:

There are so many different challenging situations: annual
meetings, ambush interviews, talk shows with your adversary sitting next to you, public hearings, and the like, I'm
not sure what their major needs are, but off the top of my
head, I would say that they need to learn how to handle
these situations a lot better.

ANALYSIS A disaster. First, you don't get an immediate
sense that the question is going to be answered (*introducing
a sense of confusion and a possible loss of attention*). Second,
the answer is a nonanswer, merely a mirror of the question.

ANSWER 2:

Three major needs come to mind: the need to understand
the enormous range of control they can exercise in such
situations, the need to define precisely what goals they
intend to accomplish, and the need to develop through
practice, experience, and systematic feedback an enhanced
sense of confidence and competence.

ANALYSIS The response had direction from the very beginning because of the definitive headline, "Three major needs
come to mind." Also, the overall response had a sense of
structure reinforced by the enumerated pattern of organization.

Is the Question Clear?

Answers hold no exclusive claim to lack of clarity. Questions can
just as easily prompt "What did you mean by that?" reactions. In
fact, the same factors that produce unclear answers also produce
unclear questions: undue length, too many concepts or facets,
jargon, highfallutin language, abstractness.

But the real question is "What are the root causes of the vague question?" Several come to mind: For instance, it is not unusual for a questioner to think he can crystallize his question by talking it out. Or, the questioner may feel torn between displaying his own knowledge and probing the depths of the respondent's mind; as a result, he presents a schizoid statement/question. In other instances, the questioner, for example, a professor, may be deliberately vague to observe the respondent's ability to focus the response. A reporter may be open-ended and vague to promote a more meandering response filled with opportunities for follow-up questions. Finally, the questioner's general communicative style may be vague and the question is just a sample of that style.

We admire Ted Koppel, Barbara Walters, and others for the insightfulness of their questions. But without clarity, how insightful would they appear to be?

Conciseness

In most Q & A situations, conciseness is a virtue, especially if it is not mistaken for curtness, defensiveness, or lack of knowledge or depth (see Chapter 6).

QUESTION TO CEO:

Do you expect this year's sales to improve over last year's?

ANSWER:

Absolutely!

ANALYSIS This concise answer

1. Communicates confidence and authority.
2. Demonstrates a respect for the audience's time (versus the "How long is he going to keep us here?" reaction).
3. Makes a response easy to follow, placing little strain on the audience's attention span.
4. Provides an opportunity for follow-up or additional questions.
5. Increases your chances of being quoted by the media— especially the electronic media.

Enough said?

GAINING AND MAINTAINING THE AUDIENCE'S ATTENTION

Gaining and maintaining the audience's attention is a primary factor in controlling your message. And while clarity and conciseness can decidedly contribute to attention, they by no means assure it. The question you are probably asking is, "What else can be done to gain and maintain the audience's attention?" Some practical advice:

Adjust your responses to your audience's frame of reference; speak their language; and refer to their experiences. This will add to your common ground and thereby enhance your credibility (see Chapter 3).

QUESTION BY A GROUP OF HOCKEY PLAYERS DURING A MEDIA INTERVIEW SEMINAR:
   Where should we look when we're appearing on a talk show? At the host? The live audience? Into the camera?
ANSWER:
   Always keep your eyes on the person who is communicating. This is similar to the way you follow the puck. Looking at the live audience during the talk show, unless they're participating, is the same as looking at your fans as you're skating down the ice.

Paint "word pictures." Help your audience visualize what you are talking about by appealing to their five senses.

QUESTION:
   What are the beaches like in St. Lucia?
ANSWER:
   Gorgeous, intimate, and immaculate. The iridescent orange sunsets are especially enticing, giving a rich golden hue to the sand and a deep turquoise glow to the warm, inviting water.

Be personal. While responding to questions, consider using expressions that project the sense that you are engaging your audience, such as "You may remember when . . . ," "How would you feel if . . . ?", and "I'm sure you know what it's like to. . . ."

Be anecdotal. By telling an anecdote well, you can paint "word pictures" and create curiosity, a major psychological stimulus to attention.

QUESTION TO ME:

When was your first contact with Ronald Reagan?

ANSWER:

In September 1978. One evening while watching TV in our bedroom, the phone rang. Upon answering it, I heard the voice say, "This is Ronald Reagan calling from California. I read your letter and decided to call rather than write." The call totally surprised me, for I had written him months earlier to ask a question for my book on political debates. Wanting to record the conversation, I asked if he wouldn't mind if I gathered my tape recorder and telephone jack (imagine my doing that today with the President of the United States). He politely said, "Yes"—without a "Well," I believe—and patiently waited until I returned. I was then able to expand the answer he had called to give me into a full interview.

ANALYSIS This answer creates and maintains attention for three principal reasons: it provides an intimate glance at a person who automatically commands interest; it is reasonably graphic; and it provokes curiosity.

PART 3

GENERAL PRINCIPLES AND TACTICS

A crucial aspect of control, especially as a respondent, is to equip your arsenal with as many potentially effective tactics as possible and to be wary of those that spell d-a-n-g-e-r. This section highlights general principles and tactics that can help you shape your response to enhance control and seize persuasive advantage.

CHAPTER 6: BUILDING YOUR RESPONSE

1. What are your major options in responding to a question?
2. Why are headlines important and what types are available to you?
3. What are the positive and negative implications of a short versus long answer?
4. What are your major options in structuring a response?
5. How do you provide proof or support for your response?

CHAPTER 7: EXPECTING THE EXPECTED

1. How should you open up a Q & A session?
2. How can you say "I don't know" without feeling—or sounding—defensive?
3. What are your major options in selecting verbal and nonverbal stalling tactics?
4. When and how should you repeat or restate a question?
5. When and how should you ask for a queston to be clarified?
6. When is "Did I answer your question?" appropriate?
7. How do you control a monopolizer?
8. How do you end a Q & A session or a media interview?

CHAPTER 6

BUILDING YOUR RESPONSE

Throughout this book, I have referred to aimless, meandering responses that undermine both the audience's comprehension and the speaker's credibility. The logical advice that follows from this concern is "Don't meander." However, this advice is useless unless we understand the factors that help prevent the perception and the reality of meandering: namely, focus, appropriate length, unity through structure and direction, support (proof), and closure.

This chapter helps you to achieve these qualities by discussing your: major response options; tactics for beginning your responses; factors in deciding how long or short your responses should be; specific patterns for structuring your response; and ways to reinforce your response with proof.

YOUR MAJOR RESPONSE OPTIONS

So far, do you feel that this book will be helpful to you?

As you are processing this question you have probably consciously or subconsciously decided that you understand it and are sorting out in your own mind whether or not you should answer this with a simple "yes" or "no," with a more exclamatory "absolutely," or "definitely not," or with an appended essay on why you regard the book as helpful or not helpful.

This is a typical, rational approach to such a question, one which highlights the first two of the following response options available to you in any situation:

Respond Only

If the question simply calls for a "yes" or "no" type response, that is all you'll provide. If you're asked for the time, you simply say it's 5:55 (without adding that dinner will be in 20 minutes). If you're asked where you work, you mention the firm, its location or both, but you don't reveal or discuss your position.

"Respond only to the question asked" is typical advice given by lawyers as they prepare witnesses, plaintiffs, and defendants for trials, and for quasi-judicial hearings. If followed, this advice reduces the risk that the person may over-answer the question, and open the proverbial "can of worms" that can invite further questioning and possibly ruin his case.

In a nonlegal context the respond-only approach may be especially credible, for it can accentuate your faithfulness to the question as you implicitly display respect for the questioner and his question. However, as you will read later in this chapter, if the response, including its tone, is too short or curt, a host of negative inferences can be drawn by your audience.

Respond and Insert

This approach involves responding first to the question and then appending an elaboration or, possibly, a totally unrelated point. In most medium-to-high-stakes Q & A exchanges, you should be on a constant lookout for openings to "bridge" from your basic response to a proactive* persuasive theme supportive of your image and substance goals.

FINANCIAL ANALYST TO PHARMACEUTICAL EXEC-
UTIVE:
>Aren't side effects responsible for the poor sales of your new anti-hypertension drug—particularly its tendency to produce nausea?

EXECUTIVE CHOOSING RESPONSE ONLY MODE:
>No.

---

* "Proactive" is a term frequently used for communication professionals to refer to the respondent's tendency to vigilantly seek openings to pursue his own goals and key messages rather than merely react to the questioner's agenda.

ANALYSIS   Too curt; generates a negative image while begging for a follow-up question.

EXECUTIVE CHOOSING RESPOND-AND-INSERT MODE:
No. In fact, the side effects are limited to a very small percentage of the user population. However, since we need to do more to get that message across, we are unfolding an aggressive, positive campaign to highlight the safety and efficacy of the drug.
ANALYSIS   Positive, active, direct, informative, and credibly confessional.

In normal conversation our approach to responding and inserting often involves an irrelevant insertion to support the stream-of-consciousness style typical of spontaneous human interaction:

WIFE TO HUSBAND:
Are you going to the office today?
HUSBAND:
No. Are we having dinner with the Davies on Friday night?
WIFE:
Yes. By the way, let the dog out before you go to Center City.

Insert and Respond

This approach is normally chosen when a comment just made by another person requires your reaction before you respond to the question just posed. It is especially common in debates and other adversarial situations in which the parties must be ready to defend themselves. This scenario from a political debate is a typical example of the insert-and-respond approach:

POLITICAL CANDIDATE A:
My opponent has done nothing to aid the homeless other than dispense his nice-sounding rhetoric. They're dying on our streets as he buries his head in the sand.
PANELIST:
What is your position regarding whether or not the city should have a greater say in the operation of our transit system?

POLITICAL CANDIDATE B:

Before I answer your question, let me clarify the record regarding my position and actions in behalf of the homeless . . .

ANALYSIS Candidate B was wise to choose the insert-and-respond tactic if the homeless issue is relevant to his target audience and if Candidate A's attack appeared persuasive or, in political debate terms, "seemed to draw blood." This choice, however, is not without risk: specifically, the risk of the moderator strictly enforcing the format as well as the risk of extending debate over a potentially damaging issue.

Insert Only

This option, an unfortunate mainstay of political communication, involves the respondent virtually ignoring the question, and taking two possible routes: actively bridging to the topic of the question without answering the question per se; or abandoning the topic entirely to discuss another issue.

Insert only is the preferred option when the question is inhospitable in content or tone, when the question is confusing, or if the respondent lacks an answer. However, of the four response options, it poses the greatest risk of inviting an embarrassing, "You didn't answer my question."

QUESTION TO A UTILITY EXECUTIVE:

Has competition in the utility industry increased appreciably over the past few years?

ANSWER:

Competition is fierce. No longer can a utility regard its service territory as inviolate—as insulated from incursions by neighboring utilities.

ANALYSIS The question per se is not answered. However, the executive actively bridges to the theme of competition. This may be a more advisable approach than, for instance, responding first by saying that he didn't know whether or not competition had increased appreciably. After all, such a response might devalue the competence or knowledge component of his credibility and thereby undermine the authority of his remarks regarding competition.

SPECIAL OPTIONS FOR ADVERSARIAL SITUATIONS

If the interaction between questioner and respondent is in any way adversarial or competitive, the level of decision-making related to responding and/or inserting becomes more complex. First, the questioner or accuser has six principal targets for attacking the respondent, his organization, or cause: Logic (usually a premise or assumption), character, motives, actions taken or not taken, credentials or record of accomplishment, and position taken on an issue.

Second, the respondent, following an accusation, has six options independent of the accuser's six targets which influence how he should pursue a decision to insert or respond: attack, counterattack, refute or defend, sell or advocate, agree (partially or fully), or ignore.

The following example illustrates how these sets of options work together in a single response:

QUESTION:
Is it true that the employee turnover rate at your company is extremely high and that your management style promotes "burnout?"

ANSWER:
Our turnover rate was, we admit, a problem. However, over the past year it has dropped 22%, placing us 10% below our industry norm. To make our environment more fulfilling, we have done a number of things. For instance, we have instituted flex-time, developed a new merit system, and recently opened a new employee Wellness Center.

ANALYSIS This answer involves a basic respond and insert approach. The headline conveys the agree option (in "Yes, but" form; see Chapter 9). The response first conveys refutation directed in defense of the company's record (the decreasing turnover rate and the industry standard comparison). The insert then carries the "sell" option focused on the company's actions to stem the turnover. The ignore option is applied to the "burnout" facet of the question (whether or not this option should have been chosen is beside the point).

In selecting these options, be especially careful not to sound too strident or defensive.[7] Just as important, whenever you are accused or challenged, seek an opportunity to present a positive message (as in the example above). If you seize this opportunity, you should be able to project an offensive versus defensive stance.

THE HEADLINE OR LEAD SENTENCE

In most Q & A situations, you should begin your answer with a headline or lead sentence—a single sentence that gives the impression you are responding to the question, even if the gist of your response will be presented as you develop your answer. The headline or lead can also communicate a sense of direction as you pursue the fuller response.

Nine principal options surround the use of the headline or lead:

The Flat Answer: "Yes." "No." "Perhaps." "Right now."

The Response (Via Agreement or Disagreement) *to a Premise Contained within the Question:* "You're right, our sales activity in this region is declining."

The Framing Statement: "There are four major reasons why we need a fare increase."

The Use of Proof: "Four fatalities within the past 18 months prove we need a light at that intersection."

The Preamble: "To understand the answer to your question, I need to supply you with a little background information."

---

[7] See Chapter 8 for a fuller discussion of this advice and the value of these options.

The Argument: "Because the government is not doing enough to shelter the homeless."

The Ricochet (Turning the Question on the Questioner): "Why did you ask that?" *or* "Why do you think I'm spending more time at the plant?"

The Editorial (Regarding the Quality or Difficulty of the Question): "You've asked a very tough question, but. . . ."

The Show of Support, Empathy, or Compassion: "I'm sorry you had difficulty with our personnel."

The better the headline or lead, the more likely that your audience will pay attention to your answer as well as sense your ability and willingness to provide it.

However, be careful not to state your argument too strongly in the headline or lead if you expect your audience to be at odds with you. Doing so can cause them to become defensive and, as a result, make them prone to refute your position internally or aloud. Therefore, instead of revealing your argument in the headline, you may wish to select one of the eight other options.

THE LONG VERSUS THE SHORT ANSWER

Once you determine your overall approach to an answer, you should decide how brief or how expanded it should be. As you do, you face a major decision that has a wide range of positive and negative implications for the clarity and interest value of your message, your strategy, and your image. In fact, length itself, regardless of the words used in your response, can transmit a variety of independent intentional or unintentional messages that can facilitate or impede the verbal message.

Implications of the Long Response

Clarity and Interest Value

Positive. The longer the response, the greater the likelihood for redundancy to clarify the point being made.

Negative. The longer response can be boring (especially if unstructured), too redundant, or too technical and devoid of examples, illustrations, anecdotes, or interesting statistics.

Tactical Implications

Positive. The longer response provides thinking time (stalling time) to produce a response and increase the perception that at least a portion of the answer may appear responsive. It also reduces the number of questions that can be asked (when active questioning is not sought), widens the opening for bridging into a proactive theme, and reduces the exposure potentially available to the opponent.

Negative. It can open Pandora's Box, laying the groundwork for damaging follow-up questions, and increases the potential for misstatements and gaffes. It provides the audience with additional time to prepare a rebuttal, and reduces the likelihood of your being quoted (if being quoted is an objective).

Image Implications

Positive. The longer response helps project your knowledge or expertise as well as your sense of cooperation, including your respect for the question, the questioner, and the audience, and in some instances projects your openness.

Negative. On the other hand, the longer response can make you appear unaware of the answer, or unwilling to provide it and, therefore, not credible because of your diversionary approach. Some longwinded answers can sound too defensive, inviting the "me thinks the maid doth protest too much" perception. In addition, your longwindedness can demonstrate insensitivity to the audience's level of interest or respect for time. Finally, a thin line often exists between longwindedness and preachiness.

Implications of the Short Response

Clarity and Interest Value

Positive. Not burdened by unnecessary verbiage, it can be more clear. It is less likely to strain the audience's attention span.

Negative. However, without sufficient elaboration, it may be too abstract.

Tactical Implications

Positive. The short response is less likely to create the traps for follow-up questions or rebuttal often produced by more lengthy responses. It provides time for more questons (if active questioning, including greater interaction with the audience, is desirable). It limits the audience's or the opponent's time to prepare a rebuttal, and increases the likelihood of being quoted (if being quoted is desirable).

Negative. Gives the opponent more potential exposure, and allows more questions to be asked (if fewer are desirable).

Image Implications

The short response can communicate confidence, directness, authority, and respect for the audience's time. However, it can also communicate too much of a "trust me" tone, caution, arrogance or aloofness, disinterest or indifference, defensiveness, a lack of knowledge or depth, or a lack of cooperation.

Inside Advice

Keep your target audience analysis in mind. Is your answer important to a key decision-maker or to your target audience? If so, you may want to provide a more developed response, *espe-*

cially if it is central to your persuasive goals. If not, it is normally advisable for you to err on the side of brevity. However, avoid being too brief; otherwise, you may invite the negative reactions described above.

Structuring the Response

I often refer to a developed response as a "mini-speech," consisting of an introduction (the headline or lead), the body or explanatory material, and a conclusion. A developed answer should reflect overall unity rather than a meandering or disjointed quality—unity to enhance both the audience's understanding and your credibility. Unity can be reinforced by four patterns of organization reflected in the following examples:

Chronological

QUESTION:
What influenced you to open your own bank?
RESPONSE:
I've been in banking most of my career. I started out as a teller in the mid-1950s, became a branch manager in the early 1960s, a regional vice president in the late 1960s, headed the consumer division in the 1970s, and was recently second in command in Radnor Trust's commercial division. My banking experience is, therefore, broad. Starting my own bank is the most fulfilling way to capitalize on that experience.

ANALYSIS Although the chronological approach was helpful to the respondent here, when choosing this approach, you must be careful to avoid providing too many chronological details, or the response can quickly become boring.

Note that the gist of the actual answer to the question comes at the end. Although one could argue justifiably that it belongs in the beginning, putting it at the end provides a good climax to the response.

Topical

QUESTION:

What influenced you to open your own bank?

RESPONSE:

Three factors. First, this is something I've always wanted to do since I entered banking 33 years ago. Second, I have broad consumer and commercial experience that I can put to fuller use by starting my own bank. Third, I received tremendous encouragement from my wife, family, and friends.

ANALYSIS The topical approach to a response is the most commonly used. Note how the "three factors" headline gives immediate structure to the response. Also note that this response is somewhat tighter than the chronological. This helps make each topical facet of the overall answer, ("something I always wanted to do," broad experience, encouragement) easy to retain.

Problem: Solution

QUESTION:

What influenced you to open your own bank?

RESPONSE:

Having lived in this area for 20 years and having spent the last 33 years in banking, I detected three clear needs for a new bank in this community: a more personalized approach to the customer, better interest rates, and greater attention to emerging small businesses. Our bank will definitely address and meet all three needs.

ANALYSIS Notice how the respondent initially builds his credentials as a banker and community member. Then note the sense of structure created by the way the need (problem) is presented. Finally note the strong close that reinforces the banker's theme. This response has unity and closure, and is the strongest business-oriented answer of the banker's three responses.

Geographical

QUESTION:
How is your marketing territory organized?
RESPONSE:
By county into three regions: Delaware, Montgomery, and Chester.

> *ANALYSIS* Although this approach is less common than the chronological or topical, it is particularly useful in explaining patterns of organization and processes.

As you think about structuring your response, you may benefit from two principles of persuasion reflected in the examples above. The first is the "anti-climax versus climax" approach to a question. "Anticlimax" involves providing the gist of your answer early, perhaps in the headline. This approach helps create a sense of immediate responsiveness and credibility, and generally makes your response more quotable for a taped TV or radio interview. However, as noted in the discussion regarding headlines, a headline that is too blunt or direct can heighten the audience's defensiveness, especially if they disagree with it. "Climax" involves building toward the gist of your response by creating a climate of curiosity or suspense (first example above). Although this approach can enhance the audience's attention, it should not be too long or appear manipulative.

The second principle of persuasion, called "primacy-recency," is reflected in the third example above. Specifically, this principle, based on extensive research, implies that we tend to remember best what we hear first and last. Therefore, in the example above, if the banker's point regarding interest rates is less significant than his points regarding personalized service (primacy) and small emerging businesses (recency), then his structural approach to the question is tactically sound.

Proof

You may remember when, during the 1988 presidential race, Pat Robertson accused George Bush's campaign of manipulating the timing of the Jimmy Swaggart sex scandal exposé to embarrass Robertson. When Robertson, a Yale Law School graduate, was asked, "Where's the proof?" he produced not a shred and seriously damaged both his campaign and his reputation.

As an arbitrator-mediator and a former college debate coach, I have studied the subject of proof or evidence closely. This study has produced the following practical advice for responding to questions:

1. If your point is controversial (especially to your target audience), be prepared to prove it via testimony, examples, data, or a real exhibit, for example, a photograph of a lung affected by heavy smoking.
2. Before you provide the proof, make sure that you sense the audience's desire for it. Otherwise, your proof, however intrinsically persuasive, could make you appear defensive.
3. If you have several "pieces" of evidence, choose only the strongest one or two, making sure they are suited to your target audience—their attitudes, interests, and patience. If they want more, let them request it.
4. Be prepared to document the source and, where appropriate, to explain the methodology behind the proof. But again, do not offer either unless your audience appears interested.
5. Take appropriate advantage of visual aids. Have charts on reserve to provide the more technical or detailed inferential proof, and photographs or actual objects to provide more "real" proof.
6. Avoid proof that may raise a skeptical eyebrow because it is not strongly relevant or is dated, lacking in authority or prestige, biased, or methodologically flawed.
7. Most important, be totally honest regarding the basic facts surrounding both the source of your proof and the proof itself.

CHAPTER 7

EXPECTING THE EXPECTED

Although fear is often associated with the unknown, it is just as often associated with not knowing how to handle a predictable situation. As a Q & A exchange approaches, you can anticipate your role in beginning and ending the exchange, as well as the awkward feeling that often accompanies declaring certain topics off limits, saying, "I don't know," stalling, requesting clarification, wondering whether or not you should ask, "Did I answer your question?" However, anticipation is of little value without proper preparation. This chapter will help you address these situations skillfully.

INVITING QUESTIONS AND SETTING THE PROPER TONE

You have just completed giving what you and your audience obviously regard as an outstanding speech. One reason for its success, apart from its insightfulness and relevance, was the energy you invested in delivering it—so much so that you feel tired. In fact, if you had your druthers, you might leave. But you can't, for a sea of hands is ready to appear as soon as you invite questions.

The manner in which you invite questions can greatly influence how the audience will perceive you in the more up-close Q & A environment, as well as the tone, quality and quantity of their questions. Your image goals play a key role in defining your tone or manner. Do you want to be approachable or aloof? Do you want to be casual or more formal? Do you want to establish a strong common bond with the audience or do you want to play the more distant expert role to the hilt? Consider these lines and the tone they suggest:

- "Are there any stupid questions?" (actually used by the superintendent of a military school)
- "John, your program chairman, told me that I should spend a few minutes answering your questions."

ANALYSIS Horrendously patronizing

- "Do you have any questions for my answers?" (used humorously by Secretary of State Henry Kissinger to open a press conference)
- "And now I'll be pleased to evade your questions." (used humorously by a friend who heads a leading Hispanic interest group)
- "I know it's hard to ask the first question, so let me begin by taking the second one." (used humorously and effectively by many speakers over the years)
- "Are there any questions?"

ANALYSIS It is better to avoid implying that there might not be—to be more positive (see the last version below),

- "And now I'll try to answer your questions."

ANALYSIS The word "try" may signal lack of confidence, although in some situations it may be appropriately humble.

- "And now I'll be pleased (delighted, happy) to answer your questions."

ANALYSIS This is more positive and generally more appropriate, although the speaker's facial expression and inflection must support the positive tone of his words.

If a positive, active Q & A session is important to you, you can actually set the tone for it within the speech itself by stating early (preferably immediately after announcing what topics or issues you plan to cover), "following my remarks, I'll look forward to your questions." Note here that the speaker subtlely shows respect for his audience by referring to their questions and not to his answers.

Announcing the Q & A within the speech itself reflects another dimension of control: It can signal the audience that the speaker prefers no interruption until the end. However, this preference may not be honored in certain situations, for example, before intensely hostile audiences and in meetings in which the norm is "question or challenge at will."

Two tactics can help prevent you from being interrupted by questions: first, if your presentation is short (e.g., under 10 minutes), you may wish to announce its approximate length as you begin, hoping your audience possesses the requisite patience to allow you to finish; second, you may choose to break a longer presentation into segments with a short Q & A exchange at the end of each segment. For example, you might break a 45-minute presentation into three 15-minute segments. (Note: The effectiveness of this approach depends largely on your ability to know when and how to end each of the exchanges. Plan in advance the lines you should choose to return to your presentation.)

OUT-OF-BOUNDS QUESTIONS

Since the Q & A exchange is frequently, if not always, a contest between whose agenda will take precedence, the questioner's or the respondent's, it's not unusual for a question to be declared out-of-bounds. The key to preventing yourself from responding to an out-of-bounds question, or to being embarrassed by not answering one, is your skill in erecting the boundaries and your ability to stick to them.

Among the more popular boundaries that can be erected at the beginning of the Q & A exchange or during it:

- "I will not comment on matter X, because it is in litigation."

COMMENT Technically, the person is not prohibited from commenting; however, whatever is said could become used in the case.

- "The question you ask is personal. Regardless of whether the answer is 'yes' or 'no,' this matter is not appropriate for this discussion."

COMMENT This type of response is occasionally used by political candidates to avoid a discussion regarding their sex lives, medial history, and financial holdings. It may not work. For instance, Gary Hary would never have gotten away with it.

- "For reasons of national security I cannot discuss this matter."

COMMENT This line, and lines like it, have been invoked by several Presidents over the years. Sometimes it has been used as a tactic to simply avoid discussing a personally embarrassing point or to avoid an "I don't know." When this occurs, the President is often accused of "wrapping himself in the flag."

- "I do not want to criticize my opponent." "Our policy is not to criticize the competition."

COMMENT This approach, called "taking the high road" is popular in politics and business. It helps convey an impression of statesmanship and confidence in one's own assets. However, it can also degenerate into an "I don't want to criticize my opponent (or my competition) but . . ."

- "Today I will answer questions only related to X, because that is my specialty."

COMMENT This approach is common in special briefings and crisis communication conferences. It helps prevent the respondent from saying, "I don't know," and the organization he or she represents from being perceived as uninformed or inadequately prepared.

- "I have answered all questions regarding this matter before. I see no point in continuing to answer these questions over and over again."

COMMENT This line seldom stifles the media. Frequently the reporter and respondent have differing views regarding what questions have and have not been answered—and how satisfactorily. This is why the media hounded Reagan and Bush about the Iran-Contra debacle for months after the issue ceased to capture front page coverage.

"I DON'T KNOW"

For several years I have administered to my clients a Communication Anxiety Survey, an instrument designed to identify their major concerns or fears as communicators. Consistently, one of the top 5 of the 33 concerns included in the survey is their fear of being caught unprepared for a question they feel that others, particularly key decision makers, think they should be able to answer.

In fact, I have seen many a politician panic before a political debate because he wasn't well versed on every issue in a briefing book containing scores of position papers. I have also seen many an executive become overwrought while preparing for a major presentation because he or she couldn't remember specific numbers related to major trends or issues.

No question about it, these concerns are rational. But the real question is, "Are they wholly rational?" Not necessarily, for often people in business, politics, and other fields who face demanding Q & A situations impose upon themselves expectations that supersede those held by their audiences.

Specific audience analysis can be an enormously helpful tool in gauging your audience's expectations of you. For example, since one of my more frequent roles is to prepare executives to appear before their boards, not only do I determine in advance the background of each board member, but I also learn as much as possible about both the types of questions each member tends to ask as well as his questioning style: Is he more prone to ask conceptual rather than specific questions? How interested is he in trends? The intricacies of finance? How tight a case does one usually need to make to convince him? To what extent has he been "presold" by other board members or executives? Is his approach to spending conservative or otherwise? How do other members of the board regard him? His questioning? And the list goes on.

If, for instance, you learn through your audience analysis that a board member is known for asking picayune questions that other board members do not especially value, you may want to spend more time studying the numbers, but with less fear of possible embarrassment if you can't instantly retrieve one in response to his question.

Or, if you learn that one of the board member's pet subjects is the effect of the changing value of the dollar on your international sales, a subject other board members are interested in, then you should prepare accordingly to reduce the likelihood of a potentially embarrassing "I don't know."

To complement setting reasonable expectations and careful preparation, objectively examine the impact an "I don't know" can have on your audience. Although it can indeed be potentially embarrassing, it can (believe it or not) also enhance your credibility. A direct, nondefensive "I don't know," especially in response to a question your audience does not *expect* you to know, can be interpreted as "I'd rather he tell us that he doesn't know than line his 'nonanswer' with bullfeathers." In fact, I have often told my clients that, ironically, an "I don't know" can actually be more credible than the actual answer, if known. (However, I certainly don't advise substituting "I don't know" for the known answer.)

Visual aids can be especially effective in limiting the likelihood of an embarrassing "I don't know" question— especially aids containing complex data or technical information. In fact, I regularly advise my clients to prepare an "on reserve" collection of visuals to support anticipated questions. However, as you retrieve the "perfect" visual to reinforce your answer, avoid transmitting the self-satisfied signal that you were just waiting for that question.

Another way to limit the potential of an "I don't know" is to create a team presentation or to have your "experts" available "on call." This approach, however, presents three risks: the risk of their not reinforcing your key messages; the risk of their contradicting you or one another on facts, arguments, or themes; and the risk of being too technical or detailed. However, through careful planning *and practice,* these risks can be abated.

Two typical companions of "I don't know" are the explanation of why you don't know and the "but I'll get the answer for you." Either or both may be helpful, but they are not without risk. In explaining why you don't know, you must be careful not to sound defensive or present a reason your audience won't accept, for example, a manager demonstrating abject ignorance about a major occurrence in his operation by using the excuse that he was on vacation.

The "I'll get the answer for you" should only be used if the information is reasonably available and not proprietary. In fact, you may be well advised to say, "I'm not sure how available that information is, but speak with me after the meeting so I will know how to contact you when I find out." This statement, in effect, lets you off the hook even further, because not only you, but your company, may not even have the information requested.

STALLING TACTICS

Do you remember the Honeymooners television series starring Jackie Gleason? If you were a regular viewer, you may recall Gleason's (as bus driver Ralph Kramden) hilarious "huma, huma, huma" stall when caught speechless in some self-imposed predicament.

Gleason's shtick merely mirrors our own sense of embarrassment when the right word or phrase temporarily or permanently eludes us—when we need more thinking time.

With characteristic ingenuity, humans have invented several verbal and nonverbal stalling tactics to provide thinking time to come up with an answer.

Verbal Stalls

"Thank you for your question" may be appropriate if not overused or gratuitously uttered following a "zinger" for which you do not feel particularly thankful.

"That's a(n) good (excellent) question (point)" may be appropriate reinforcement, especially in a teaching situation. However, it may also sound patronizing and unduly judgmental. It may make other questioners who were not reinforced in this manner feel that their questions were not as good. If the question contains a premise damning you, your cause, or your point of view, the positive reinforcement "That's a good point" could make the audience sense that the questioner's claim may be valid. Moreover, they may sense that you are acquiescing to the questioner's point of view too easily or too gratuitously. As a substitute, "that's interesting" or "intriguing" may sound more genuine and be less prone to elicit the negative reactions described above.

"I'm glad you asked that question" may be and sound genuine. However, I have frequently seen it expressed when the questioner would have paid money to prevent the question from being asked. This approach can sound more genuine (while you simultaneously extend your stall) by explaining briefly why you're "glad," for example, "because it focuses on a significant issue facing all of us."

"Let me take a moment to think about your question is one of the more genuine stalls." In fact, it has a confessional tone that can relieve some of the stress related to the question. However, be sure that your stall or pause is not too long—no more than nine months pregnant.

"That's a tough (difficult) question is another more genuine stall." Psychologically, it, in a sense, compliments the questioner by acknowledging a challenging question and provides the respondent with cathartic or confessional relief in admitting to its difficulty. The relief may also clear the way for a quality response.

The temporarily postponed answer: "I'll be covering that issue shortly." In certain situations, this tactic may be acceptable, especially if your presentation is interrupted by a question. However, if a key target-audience member is asking the question, your temporarily postponed answer could lead not only to the defeat of your proposal, but also to a permanently postponed raise or promotion.

Beyond knowing your audience, the key to making the temporarily postponed answer work for you is your tone; it should not be austere, but friendly.

"Let me first ask you a question before I answer yours." Sometimes this may be a legitimate and positively perceived stalling tactic, especially if the answer to the question asked by the respondent appears reasonably necessary to responding to the initial question.

QUESTION ASKED BY ONE OF MY CLIENTS:

Should I take a glass of water to the lectern when I speak?

QUESTION I ASKED IN RESPONSE:

Do you tend to get dry mouth when you speak?

"I'm frequently asked that question." If you are, why announce it? First, it tells the questioner that his query is not fresh or original. Second, you are diminishing your credibility and the credibility of your response by signaling the audience that "you're ready for this one." Third, if the question criticizes you or your position in any way, signaling the audience that it is "frequently asked" may cause them to feel that the criticism has merit—that they may have reason to jump onto the (negative) bandwagon.

"As I said earlier. . . ." Although this may occasionally be appropriate, be careful that it isn't "code" for "if you were listening." Otherwise, this defensive putdown can damage your rapport with your audience.

Beginning with an essay until the answer surfaces is the most frequent type of stall. Your main concern here should be not to meandor; otherwise the audience may realize that you are evading because you don't know the answer or are embarrassed by it.

"Well." A classic Ronald Reagan stall. During preparations for the debate with Jimmy Carter, one of Reagan's long-time advisors asked me if Reagan's frequent use of "Well" caused me concern. My answer: "Well, I don't think we should tamper with it. Otherwise, he could become too self-conscious about saying 'well' and become distracted from both the question and the answer."

Repeating the Question

Repeating the question is generally advisable only if a portion of your audience can't hear you. If you repeat the question and everyone heard it the first time, then you will probably be branding yourself as a transparent staller (this is especially true when dealing with a small audience). If, however, it appears that a portion of the audience did not hear the question, you are entitled to a double stall: first by asking if you should repeat the question (2 to 5 seconds), and then by repeating it.

Repeating a question loaded with hostile language directed at you can make you look ridiculous unless you can repeat it in an appropriately humorous manner or by ridiculing the questioner (without creating the "boomerang effect"). Usually, however, it is more advisable to rephrase the question.

In friendly situations, repeating a short question may be an acceptable stall. One good example involves a recent interview between a TV reporter and the first professional female baseball umpire:

REPORTER:

Do you regard yourself as a saint? (for breaking the sex barrier to umpiring)

FEMALE UMPIRE:

Do I consider myself a saint? No. Don't you know that all umpires are supposed to be the devil?

Restating the Question

Restating the question may be advisable to put it in more manageable form. That is, the question may be too long or confusing, or contain a premise or facet you intend to avoid.

However, especially when appearing before decision-makers, be careful not to alter a question's intent when restating it.

Requesting Clarification

"Would You Please Clarify Your Question?" At first blush, it may seem only sensible to ask for a question to be clarified if you sincerely don't understand it. After all, you don't want to risk any possible embarrassment related to misunderstanding or not answering the question. Moreover, by asking for the question to be clarified, you are also buying yourself more thinking time.

One effective way to ask for clarification is to identify the terms or section of the question you did not understand. For example, "I'm not sure I understand what you mean by 'the time horizon for cost effectiveness to diminish.' " By choosing this active listening approach, you are signaling the questioner and the audience that you intend to be responsive.

However, asking for clarification also has its risks—risks that can prompt one to produce a tangential response rather than a faithful one. For instance, if the questioner is hostile, long-winded, or both, your request for clarification may result in an expanded diatribe and an even more difficult—and unclear —question. In addition, in live radio and TV interviews and political debates, such a request may signal the interviewee's lack of knowledge or, worse yet, weak intelligence, especially if the question seems clear to the audience.

One of the ploys frequently used by respondents when fielding an obviously "fuzzy" question is not to ask for clarification, but to begin instead with the disclaimer: "I'm not sure I fully understand your question, but I'll give it a try." This can help let you off the hook, especially if you are later accused of not having understood or answered the question.

Nonverbal Stalls

Nonverbal stalls, which can be used in combination with verbal stalls, are often more subtle.

Taking a drink of water as the question is asked, or immediately after, is generally acceptable, unless you're doing it too frequently. If so, you may be leading up to the Grand Stall—an unplanned trip to the men's or ladies' room.

Lighting a pipe, cigar, or cigarette was formerly more acceptable. With taboos on smoking, especially on cigarettes and cigars, choosing this stall should be based on a careful analysis of your audience.

Removing eyeglasses can connote a more reflective mode. However, I have seen many participants in my Q & A seminars overuse this ploy—so much so that an accelerated videotape replay shows their glasses repeatedly coming on and off with the cadence of a Charlie Chaplin movie.

Taking a few steps toward the questioner as the question is ending or immediately after it is asked can be natural and engaging. However, be careful not to "overengage" a hostile questioner or to invade your questioner's "space."

Returning to a visual aid is a terrific stall as long as the aid is relevant and well prepared.

One final point regarding the stall: Don't overreact to the momentary silence between the asking of the question and your response. In fact the silence created by your pause—if not protracted—can not only give you added thinking time, but it can also signal your thoughtfulness (versus glibness) and respect for the questioner.

"Did I Answer Your Question?"

In a teaching situation, this question may be appropriate, especially when interacting with a student who appears reluctant to provide feedback or ask for clarification. In most other situations, however, it is not advisable. For example, in a public hearing, crisis news conference, or annual meeting where the climate is growing increasingly hostile, asking "Did I answer your question?" can result in an unsettling chorus of "Nos" possibly followed by the same question restated or by one from another questioner.

"Did I answer your question?" not only relinquishes your control, but it can also signal a lack of confidence in your response, a cue you normally would not want to transmit to your superiors, decision makers, or to the media.

When facing a nonhostile situation, what do you do when your answer is central to your persuasive goal and you are not receiving reinforcing feedback from your audience? Instead of asking "Did I answer your question?" you may be better served by, "Would you like me to elaborate?" or, "If you wish, I'd be pleased to develop this further." These lines, if delivered without a hint of tentativeness, can replace a possible perception of lack of confidence with one of confidence and appropriate respect for the audience.

TACTICS FOR THE TEAM PRESENTATION

A fair measure of my consulting practice is devoted to preparing people to make team presentations, whether they are addressing an internal meeting, a current or prospective client, a group of convention or seminar attendees, or making a media appearance, for example, participating in a talk show or news conference.

Successful team presentations require a consistent theme and set of key messages, a sense of unity among the presenters and the presentations, the absence of unnecessary repetition, and smooth handling of the Q & A (as the following example clarifies):

As the CEO of the Haddonfield Hat Company, you, your COO, and your CFO have decided you should appear before an influential group of financial analysts to convince them of the attractiveness of your firm as an investment.

Specifically, you plan to persuade them that "hats are back" and that you have the fiscal strength, marketing savvy, and manufacturing support to sustain this trend. As you field their questions, you need to be facile in handling three tactics: *the handoff, the piggyback play,* and *blowing the whistle on your own teammates*.

The Handoff

This tactic involves delegating a response. As you do, you have two options: first, to provide a basic answer before asking your colleague to provide the details—an option that highlights your knowledgeability and thereby your competence; second, to introduce your colleague in a manner that clarifies why he is in a better position to provide the answer or elaboration. As you hand the ball off, avoid appearing defensive, especially when you do not know the answer.

The "sticky ball" is an interesting variation of the hand-off. Suppose you are asked why a major line of hats failed—a predictably tough question. Although you can answer the question fully, you hand it off to the COO to distance yourself from the failure.

The sticky ball is fraught with risks. The analysts could perceive you to be "sticking" the sticky ball to your COO. Moreover, unless the COO agreed in advance to field this question, he may be so miffed with you that he decides to bolt Haddonfield Hat and form the Camden Chapeau Company.

The Piggyback Play

Your COO has done a nice job responding to an important question regarding your advertising campaign: however, he left out one big point that prompts you to "piggyback" onto his answer. As you do, make sure you are using the right line:

1. "Joe failed to make one important point."

ANALYSIS This response showcases your team by declaring their failures, which invites the disrespect of the analysts and your colleagues.

2. "Let me add to what Joe has said by. . . ."

ANALYSIS Fine

3. "Joe's answer reminded me of an additional point."

ANALYSIS Perfect (if fully honest).

The execution of the handoff and the piggyback play can be smoother if the participants decide in advance who will be mainly responsible for which topics. However, during the actual exchange, be careful not to tune out a question apparently intended for another team member. Despite the division of labor, you may be required to answer it or to comment on it following an initial answer. Again, quality listening is key!

"Blowing the Whistle" on Your Own Teammate

Your COO has just declared that a new and promising line of hats will appear in the fall. However, he means spring. What do you do? Regardless of his position, *gently* blow the whistle to correct him, especially if the misstatement relates to an important issue. You may simply interrupt and say, "Joe, you mean spring," or wait until he finishes and say, "Joe, you meant to say spring," or "Joe meant to say spring." Humor may even be appropriate to relieve the tension produced by the misstatement: "Joe is more enthusiastic about this line of hats than I realized; he's moved us up by two seasons." Be careful, though, that the humor is not too heavily laced with a put-down tone.

CONTROLLING THE MONOPOLIZER

We've all seen situations in which a questioner either holds the speaker at bay with a long-winded question or continues to ask questions while effectively excluding others. These situations challenge the respondent's control. To exercise the proper amount of control in these situations, regardless of whether or not the questioner is hostile, you have several options. If the questioning is getting too long-winded (as evidenced particularly by the audience's nonverbal cues), you may need to: (1) interrupt with "I understand your question;" (2) restate the question, capturing the gist of it—or the "spin" you wish to place on it; or (3) request clarification, for example, "Please briefly clarify (or summarize) your question."

Note: This third option is risky since it could relinquish even more floor time to the monopolizer. However, if you've really lost the train of the monopolizer's question, you may have little choice.

If the monopolizer is posing questions too frequently, you may need to work harder at attempting to balance the participation. For example, you might explain, without being too harsh, that other people have questions as well. You may also want to add that you will try to get back to him or her after you have responded to questions posed by other audience members. You may offer a private meeting following the engagement or at a later date. This, of course, works only when other people are trying to pose questions.

If, however, the monopolizer is a key target-audience member, silent prayer may be your best approach.[8]

KNOWING WHEN AND HOW TO END

A terrific speaking engagement, news conference, or media interview can quickly turn into a disaster if it runs on for too long. Not only might the audience's patience be taxed, but the risks of generating unnecessary controversy, making a misstatement, and not ending your performance on a positive note can be increased.

The issue, once again, is control. Specifically, how much of it is available to you directly, or through others? Consider these options.

Ending the Outside Speaking Engagement

You may ask the program chairman to inform the audience that you will be available for a Q & A session of approximately X minutes following your speech. You may also request that he explain why you can't stay longer, for example, you have "a plane to catch," another meeting, etc.

In establishing the length of the Q & A, you may want to offer somewhat less time than what is actually available (without appearing too ungenerous). This gives you the option to expand the Q & A session. If this occurs, your additional time with the audience can be regarded as a bonus, one that can boost

---

[8] Also refer to Chapter Nine for additional advice regarding how to control hostile questioners and monopolizers at heavily attended meetings.

your credibility, particularly through the components of cooperation and compatibility.

Do make sure that the program chairman understands that he, not you, is to end the session. You do not want to be perceived as "leaving the host's table prematurely." However, to make sure that the program doesn't go on any longer than necessary, consider establishing with the program chair a nonverbal signal system. For instance, you may give him a quick look either when it's time to end the program, or to inform the audience that you will answer only one, two, or three more questions.

Before you leave the stage to mingle or catch that plane, do your best to end on a positive note. If the last question was negative and your answer was not especially positive or strong, field one more question if the audience seems supportive of both you and the additional question. Alternatively, you may want to arrange for the last question to be a plant. If so, make sure that it is not a patent plant (e.g., the CEO's wife); they don't go over well on most audiences.

An important option for ending your program is the mini-speech, a recap of the major ideas discussed during the Q & A that tie in with your persuasive goals. To illustrate this option, imagine that you are about to complete your appearance before a public zoning hearing where you have advocated a 150,000-foot expansion of your factory in the face of active, tough questioning.

> This evening you have asked a lot of questions that reflect your understandable interest in protecting your rights and the attractiveness of your neighborhood. You have asked about a smokestack, and I have assured you that there won't be one. You have asked about our building design, and I have shown you our plans to blend it into the environment. You have asked about additional traffic, and I have assured you that it will be minimal. There isn't a question or concern that I haven't addressed. We have proven over the years that we want to be a good neighbor and we will do everything reasonable to continue to be one. I ask for your support.

Your final option in ending the Q & A exchange involves expressing the appropriate amenities: "Thank you" (appropriate for most situations); "I found your questions most enlightening;" "I wish you a most productive and enjoyable conference;" "Plan to visit us if you're in our area" etc. In delivering lines such as these, be sure to *feel and sound genuine* and to display full eye contact.

PART IV

SPECIAL CHALLENGES

So many of the people who seek our counsel ask us "How should I field tough, trick and hostile questions?" "How do I handle a hostile audience?" "What do I do if I invite questions and none are asked?" As the list below indicates, this section addresses these concerns practically and comprehensively.

CHAPTER 8: FIELDING TOUGH, TRICK, AND HOSTILE QUESTIONS

1. What are the ingredients of Ronald Reagan's Teflon?
2. Where do "banana peels" come from?
3. What are the major types of banana peels and how can they be fielded?

CHAPTER 9: MANAGING HOSTILITY

1. How should we analyze the supposed presence of hostility in an audience?
2. What factors promote the audience's hostility?
3. How can you prevent yourself from overreacting to hostility?
4. What tactics can you use to manage hostility?

CHAPTER 10: COMBATTING SILENCE

1. What factors promote no questions during a Q & A session?
2. How can the format restrict or facilitate Q & A?
3. What is the influence of management's tone on the Q & A session?
4. What tactics can you use to make the Q & A session more facilitative?

CHAPTER 8

FIELDING TOUGH, TRICK, AND HOSTILE QUESTIONS

THE SCENE:
Democratic presidential candidate and frontrunner Gary
Hart at a news conference held in May 1987 (following a
major news story that, although he was married, he had
spent the previous weekend with Donna Rice, a voluptuous
28-year-old model).
THE QUESTION:
Have you ever committed adultery? [one of dozens posed]
HART'S ANSWER:
A self-incriminating refusal to respond.
THE RESULT:
Within 72 hours, his soaring candidacy plummeted and
ended with enormous public disgrace, followed 6 months
later by another ill-fated campaign.

THE SCENE:
Al Campanis, executive for 44 years with the Brooklyn
Dodgers, appearing on ABC's Nightline with Host Ted
Koppel on the 40th anniversary of Dodger Jackie Robin-
son's entry as the first black into the major leagues.
KOPPEL'S QUESTION:
Why are there so few blacks in baseball management?
CAMPANIS' ANSWER:
I truly believe that they may not have some of the necessi-
ties to be, let's say, a field manager, or perhaps a general

manager. . . . Well, I don't say all of them, but they certainly are short. How many quarterbacks do you have—how many pitchers do you have that are black?

THE FOLLOWUP:

Koppel tried to bail him out with follow-up questions, but Campanis kept misspeaking, asking and answering his own question as the fatal blow: "Why aren't black men, or black people, good swimmers? Because they don't have the buoyancy. [a tired myth]

THE RESULT:

Within 24 hours, Campanis apologized, but within 48 hours, the 44-year veteran was fired.

THE SCENE:

The Senate Caucus Room, Washington, D.C., July 7, 8, 9, 10, 13, 14, 1987. The witness: Colonel Oliver North, to many the "fall guy" for the Iran-Contra Arms-for-Hostages fiasco, breaks his eight-month silence by testifying with limited immunity.

THE QUESTION:

3,137 questions and answers over the 6-day period.

THE RESULT:

With enormous composure, a compelling presence, and powerful persuasive resourcefulness, North instantly became a national hero.

Three different situations. Three different results. Yet there were commonalities as well. Hart, Campanis and North were all highly competent figures in their respective fields. Most important, the fate of each of them was sealed by the manner in which they handled the challenge presented by the question-and-answer situation they faced. Hart and Campanis failed miserably—Hart because he misbehaved so badly that nothing would have helped him, Campanis because he misspoke ("misthought" and misprepared). North, however, could not have done better; he mesmerized the American people and, as a result, won their support for his cause, their contributions to his legal defense fund, and most notably, their hearts.

As we analyze these events, all occurring within 3 short

months, we can also conclude that while North was clearly well prepared, Hart and Campanis were both victimized by the surprise that comes from not being prepared. Yes, it can take years of hard work to make one's star rise, yet it can fall immediately—and sometimes irreversibly—because of one misdeed or misstatement.

The obvious message here is to prevent surprises through careful planning and practice. The less obvious message is that specific approaches are available to you to counter the element of surprise created by a hostile, tough, or entrapping question.

TEFLON

The DuPont Company patented it. Ronald Reagan perfected it and capitalized on it (especially during his first term). His capacity to deflect a question or comment, however tough or penetrating, and keep the audience on his side will remain one of the long-remembered assets that contributed to the well-deserved epithet "The Great Communicator." As George Will remarked, Reagan is the only person who can "walk into a room, have the ceiling fall on him, and walk out without a fleck of plaster in his hair." Most notably, few people will forget Reagan's simple and spontaneous use of the line, "There you go again" to deflect Jimmy Carter's forceful denunciation of Reagan's position regarding national health policy.

Wouldn't it be nice if we could purchase a can of Reagan Teflon that could envelop us with an impenetrable film to help repel potentially embarrassing questions. We know the ingredients of Reagan Teflon (listed below); we simply don't now how to can them.

Ingredients of Teflon (The Reagan Version)

- Popularity with the people.
- An affable, avuncular manner.
- A quick wit, a good overall sense of humor (including the capacity not to take one's self too seriously).
- A winning smile.

- A soothing voice.
- The capacity to sense the inherent danger/risk in a question.
- The ability to dodge and obfuscate artfully.
- The ability to memorize or compose on-the-spot compelling lines that capture the essence of his position.
- The capacity to maintain composure under duress ("grace under fire").
- An aura of respectability generated by age.
- An aura of respectability generated by the position and the resulting deference of others.
- An ability and widely acknowledged commitment to American values.

Any attempt to blend these 12 ingredients into a workable formula suited to someone else would be impossible, if not ridiculous (unless in preparation for a Ronald Reagan imitation). In fact, using any single ingredient of Reagan's Teflon often requires enormous self-understanding, patience, and practice. If one does not smile easily, trying to smile like Reagan in any kind of an engagement can become an immediate disaster. The same goes for a sense of humor. If a person doesn't have one, 100 private lessons with Ronald Reagan, Johnny Carson, or Bob Hope are not likely to produce one. However, on the more positive side, we can cultivate the ability to communicate shared values (for example, desire to succeed, love for family, loyalty to country, honesty, fairness, compassion, etc.). And we can learn how to control our composure. Or, at least most of us can.

BANANA PEELS

The "banana peels" approach to handling tough, trick, and entrapping questions is one method anyone can learn and develop. It was created by me for Ronald Reagan's debates with John Anderson and Jimmy Carter during the 1980 presidential race. Since then, the approach has been refined considerably and has been used widely in numerous situations besides debates: highly challenging presentations, media interviews, crisis situations, annual meetings, public hearings, etc.

The term banana peels takes its name from an incident (perhaps apocryphal) involving a G.I. who was returning home without a scratch from the front lines following World War II. As his family greeted him on the front steps, he slipped on a banana peel and broke his leg.

The banana peels approach is based on four premises: (1) Most—if not all—tough questions can be placed in the following twelve banana peel categories; (2) Any trick, tough, or hostile question can actually contain more than one type of banana peel; (3) A set of distinct tactical response options applies to each type of banana peel; (4) The executive can avoid slipping on banana peels by learning the categories and response options (including the special options discussed on page 81).

Banana Peel 1: The Hostile Question

The hostile question can be one of the toughest. Not only does it seek to elicit information, it is often intended to create embarrassment. Here the respondent's ego is placed on the alert—often resulting in undue defensiveness or loss of composure (see Chapter 3).

Although executives tend to regard hostile questions as risky, if skillfully addressed, they can be filled with opportunity. How better can a respondent display the ability to think quickly and project command and composure than under the pressure produced by hostile questions?

Hostile Banana Groves

The key to handling hostile questions—and to avoiding stepping on all types of banana peels—is to anticipate them. Therefore, where do hostile banana peels originally come from? From hostile banana groves. The banana groves approach helps you anticipate the more predictable lines of questioning related to a hostile Q & A exchange. The three major types of groves are described and illustrated here:

HOSTILE BANANA GROVE A: QUESTIONS
REGARDING ACTIONS

1. Acted in the absence of a clear and present need.

   Example: Why did you build a $40 million office center when there is a glut of high quality, conveniently located and reasonably priced space?

2. Acted without sufficient information.

   Example: Why did you take a position on the Supreme Court nominee when you admit yourself that you haven't even reviewed his major cases?

3. Acted without sufficient planning.

   Example: Why isn't the new telephone system you selected adaptable to forecasted technological advances?

4. Acted too slowly (decisional paralysis).

   Example: Isn't the main reason why we lost this account because you and your team dragged your feet?

5. Acted too quickly.

   Example: Why didn't you wait the extra week to receive the proposal from American Machine? It could have saved us nearly $500,000.

6. Acted without sufficient attention to input from important constituencies.

   Example: Don't you think that if we had listened more carefully to the customer that we wouldn't be in this mess?

7. Acted without sufficient attention to quality or safety considerations.

   Example: Wouldn't we have been able to prevent the return of these thousands of worn discs if we had made them slightly thicker?

8. Picked or kept the wrong people.

   Example: No wonder our accounts are down. How can you expect a new MBA with no practical marketing experience to handle them? Any day I'd trade a prestigious degree and a high I.Q. for a background with solid experience and results.

9. Acted contrary to assurances, past practice, established standards.
   Example: Why didn't you alert me to the possibility of a cost overrun? You told me repeatedly that you would.
10. Acted without sufficient oversight or supervision.
    Example: Don't you feel that if you had paid closer attention to the training needs of the nuclear power station control room operators that we could have avoided this crisis?
11. Acted without heeding the warning signals.
    Example: The maintenance record on the brake system of that school bus that crashed indicates that you took a band-aid approach to the problem instead of replacing the whole system. Why?
12. Acted too harshly (or leniently).
    Example: Why did you fire John, a good worker, simply because he was arrested for possessing a very small amount of marijuana?

Hostile Banana Grove B: Questions Regarding Motives

1. Acted out of financial selfishness.
   Example: As a shareholder, I'd like to know how you and your executive team can reward yourselves with such a handsome stock option plan when the financial results of this company have been abominable?
2. Acted out of a need for greater control.
   Example: As a board member I feel obligated to tell you that some of us feel that the reason you fired Pollak was because you regarded him as a potential threat to your position. How do you react to this?
3. Acted out of a need for a higher profile/greater visibility.
   Example: As a board member, I am interested in knowing how you react to the allegation that your decision to appear in our company's television commercials is driven more by your own political ambitions than by your commitment to your present position?

Hostile Banana Grove C: Questions Regarding Character

1. Deceived or lied.
   Example: Your resume indicates that you graduated from Plato University. Yet in checking with their registrar and with their alumni association, they have no record of you. Did you change you name, or are you trying to pull the wool over our eyes?
2. Took improper advantage.
   Example: You requested that we underwrite your trip to the national convention, and yet according to informed sources, you didn't attend one session. In fact, you apparently spent most of the time touring and carousing. How do you explain this?
3. Attempted to "cover up."
   Example: Why were we not informed, as we should have been, that the temperature of the (nuclear) fuel rods had risen well above normal levels and that you had to take emergency action to cool them down?
4. Divulged proprietary information.
   Example: The only way our competition could have learned about our "surprise" advertising blitz had to be through a leak in your operation. Whom do you suspect? What do you think we should do about it?
5. Conducted oneself in an improper/immoral manner.
   Example: Did you, without our consent, and contrary to both our policy and established law, bribe the purchasing agent of Ficticco to secure your most recent order?
6. Reneged on a commitment/promise.
   Example: You promised the union an active role in developing with management an employee drug testing program, and yet you acted on your own. Why? How can we assign any credibility to your words or actions when you can't keep a simple promise?

Now that you have examined the three banana groves, a question that may be occurring to you is, "Are these questions hostile, or are they simply tough?" In most instances, the answer would be "both." Not only do they constitute potentially formidable challenges to the executive's actions, motives, or character, they also involve situations conducive to spawning hostility.

Handling the Toughest Banana Peel—The Hostile Question

The first key to handling a hostile question is emotional control. The more the executive can control his emotions—including his ego and capacity not to take a "hostile" remark too personally— the better. In fact, as explained in Chapters 3 and 9, emotional control or composure can be as important as, if not more important, than content.

The second key to handling a hostile question is quality listening. Emotions can seriously interfere with our ability to listen. A controversial facet of a multifaceted hostile question or an emotion-laden accusation can produce an immediate short circuit in the listening process, weakening your ability to provide a quality response. Therefore, listen carefully, paying close attention to the words, the *apparent* intent (trying to gauge the questioner's "hidden agenda" can often impair quality listening), and the stated and unstated assumptions.

The third key to handling a hostile question is quality dissection. Quality dissection involves analyzing the language and assumptions of a question and framing a response around the analysis. It can occur only following effective listening.

EXAMPLE   "How do you expect more business with your *rotten* customer service record?"

ASSUMPTION DISSECTION

1. You expect more business.
   Analysis: May be true or untrue.
2. Your customer service record is "rotten."
   Analysis: May be fair or unfair.
3. The customer service record is a significant factor in generating more business.
   Analysis: May be true or untrue. Many customers (e.g., mail order) are not aware of a company's customer service record.

LANGUAGE DISSECTION
  "Rotten"
ANALYSIS Accusation may stand if not refuted. However, it may be reinforced if refuted too defensively. For example, if you say, "Our record is not rotten" and sound too defensive and do not convincingly prove the contrary, you could end up inadvertantly supporting the questioner (the "boomerang effect"). Moreover, you might be repeating the word "rotten" for an audience that didn't hear/note it when the question was asked. Hence, you could end up "poisoning your own well."

Another option in responding to a hostile question is to ignore a term (e.g., "rotten"), a hostile facet (in a multifaceted question), or an assumption. Two reasons stand behind this option: Either you don't have a good answer, or the answer you have, while technically sound, will impede your persuasive advances because of its tone or complexity.

Persuasive Advances

Remember when handling a hostile question that the name of the game is persuasion—specifically, your principal purpose is to advance your persuasive substance and image goals. Therefore, if your "rotten" record is unfairly challenged and truth is on your side, you should bridge as deftly as possible to a genuinely positive (versus a negative or defensive) response:

> We are proud of our customer service record. Despite an occasional grievance, which any business experiences, we receive exceptionally strong feedback from our customers—directly and from the surveys we conduct. They perceive us as attentive and efficient, two reasons why our sales have increased by at least 15% annually for the past 5 years.

Banana Peel 2—The Speculative Question

The speculative question is one of the easiest to spot, because it automatically calls for the speaker to make a prediction.

> EXAMPLE   To a sales manager: "What do you expect your sales to be next year?"

ANALYSIS

1. If you overestimate, you may be eventually creating a perceived slump or shortfall.
2. If you underestimate, you might be creating a perceived boon (not necessarily positive, for it can confuse planning and expectations).
3. If you refuse to answer or ignore the question, you might be sending an inadvertent message declaring low confidence in your sales.
4. And, finally, if you find exacting numerical predictions risky (as in the examples above) a positive, proactive theme line is the bare minimum response you should consider: "We expect sales to continue to increase steadily next year."

EXAMPLE To a coach: "Will your team make it to the playoffs?"

ANALYSIS

- If you say "Yes" too pointedly, you could communicate and instill overconfidence in your team.
- If you say "No" or communicate too much doubt, you could jeopardize morale, not to speak of attendance and gate receipts.
- If you indicate "Yes" and those clearly in the know (including the team and the front office) think "No way," then you are at best a dreamer and at worst a liar.
- If you do have a shot at the playoffs and you highlight the resourcefulness of the team coupled with favorable extraneous factors (e.g., other teams in the running not doing well) you will probably score—at least in your answer.

As you tackle a speculative question, don't hesitate to use such expressions as "I'd rather not speculate," "I make it a practice not to speculate," or "Although you are asking me to speculate, let me try to answer your question." By using such expressions you are, in effect, presenting a disclaimer that might help keep you off the hook—or the hot seat.

My favorite disclaimer line surfaced during one of my recent seminars. An executive was asked to predict stock market performance for the following year. His response: "I no longer make public my crystal ball gazing because I am tired of eating crushed glass."

Banana Peel 3—The Hypothetical Question

The hypothetical question is tricky, for it invites the respondent to take a position based on one or more hypothetical assumptions.

EXAMPLE (with one hypothetical assumption) "If sales increase within the next year, would you still propose cutting the advertising budget?"

ANALYSIS

- Do you expect sales to increase next year? If you do, you may wish to state proactively that you expect them to. If you do not, you may wish to challenge the assumption or to remind the audience that it is "merely hypothetical."
- On the other hand, you may not necessarily agree with the assumption that a causal connection should exist between sales volume and advertising expenditures. Therefore, you may wish to respond solely to this misassumption.
- If you agree with both assumptions, then your answer is a piece of cake—a "Yes" or "No" plus any embellishment you may wish to add.

EXAMPLE (with three hypothetical assumptions) "Say we acquire Panacea Pharmaceuticals and merge both our and their research and development and domestic sales divisions. Wouldn't the efficiencies that should result from this consolidation significantly strengthen our financial performance?"

ANALYSIS

1. *Re:* hypothetical assumption A: "Is the acquisition of Panacea Pharmaceuticals a realistic possibility?" If not, challenge this assumption and the response should normally go no further.
2. *Re:* hypothetical assumption B: "Is the merger of the research and development efforts a realistic possibility?" If not, you may challenge this assumption.
3. *Re:* hypothetical assumption C: "Is the merger of the domestic sales division a realistic possibility?" If not, here's another opportunity to challenge the assumption.
4. *Re:* independent assumptions:
   "The combined mergers will contribute to efficiencies." Is this causal claim valid? If not, it may need to be challenged.
   "The efficiencies will 'significantly strengthen' financial performance." Again, is this causal claim valid? If not, a challenge may again be appropriate.

This Panacea Pharmaceuticals example highlights the trickiness of hypothetical questions. Although it took only 15 seconds to pose this question, it is laced with five interdependent assumptions—a challenge for even the most facile respondent.

As you field such "banana peels," you can also rely on such trusty disclaimers as, "Although your question is hypothetical, I'll do my best to answer it," or, "I'd rather not play Monday-morning quarterback," a handy line when you're asked to second guess an action already taken.

EXAMPLE   If you had read this book before that Q & A exchange, don't you think you would have done better?

ANALYSIS While you and I know that the truthful answer is "absolutely," the Monday-morning quarterback line may be (as I swallow a bit of author's pride) the better face-saver.

Banana Peel 4—The Picayune/Overspecific Question

Unlike speculative or hypothetical questions, picayune questions do not normally challenge our reasoning processes. Rather, they challenge our memory banks. Few of us are, in the words of S. J. Perelman, "afflicted with total recall." Yet too many of us feel embarrassed if we cannot instantly retrieve an elusive number or fact from our cerebral computers.

Command of numbers and details can be enormously impressive. However, I have advised scores of persons who can retain and recite the numbers, but who can't define the point they make. For example, if you don't understand baseball, being told that Ted Williams hit .406 in 1941 will probably draw an unsettling yawn instead of the intended "Wow!"

> EXAMPLE   (one that I'm frequently asked)   "What is the percentage of your corporate vs. political business during election years?"
>
> *ANALYSIS*
>
> 1. During the past election year it was approximately two-thirds corporate and one-third political (but I don't know the exact number).
> 2. Furthermore, the question asked about "years." The truth is that I hadn't carefully tracked these percentages before the past election. Therefore, I would unhesitatingly give the "two-thirds/one-third" answer. Then, depending on my target audience's interest in the question, I would decide whether or not to explain that I hadn't tracked earlier percentages.

When you're stuck and don't have the requested number at your fingertips, you have five major choices that may be used separately or in combination:

1. Offer to make the number available as soon as reasonably possible (if conveniently accessible and not proprietary or embarrassing).

2. Present the trend with the specific figures (increase, decrease, etc.).
3. Say nondefensively that you don't have the exact figure.
4. Indicate that the figures are either proprietary (not a good move if your boss is making the request) or that they are difficult to access.
5. Pass the ball to a colleague who "works more closely with this issue."

In the final analysis, although you should demonstrate reasonable command of the numbers or facts most pertinent to your position, in many instances you may be better served by remembering your anniversary date and your spouse's birthday.

Banana Peel 5—The Leading Question

We can all think back to the days of Perry Mason or another favorite television courtroom lawyer who would confidently object to a question because it was leading the witness. But wouldn't you agree that we probably have less clear recollections of where we might have been trapped by a leading question? (Were you just trapped?)

The leading question, by its very nature, imposes the questioner's assumptions on you as respondent, often making it difficult for you to find an out.

> EXAMPLE (boss to employee) "Bob (the new president) has done a great job instilling new life into this company, hasn't he?"

> *ANALYSIS*

1. You may immediately agree.
2. You may not feel that Bob has done a great job, but a good or decent job. Therefore, you have three choices:
   a. You may simply want to say "yes" to avoid the issue.
   b. You may question what your boss meant by "great" (choosing to do so may depend on your relationship with him or her).

c. You may wish to substitute your own term, for example, "decent."
3. You may disagree.
4. You may deflect (ignore) the actual question by simply mentioning one or more of Bob's qualities or actions you do like.
5. You may choose to accept the expression "instilling life," or ask that it be defined.
6. You may or may not choose to mention—possibly with a smile—that the question is leading.

Banana Peel 6—The Loaded Question

The loaded question, as most of the banana peels discussed so far, is normally filled with assumptions. However, these assumptions are often accusatory, and, if unnoticed, could produce a monumental slip.

EXAMPLE "Why hasn't your company been able to attract more business with one of the best management teams in the nation?"

ANALYSIS

Assumption 1: (Accusation) Your company has not attracted business as it should.
Assumption 2: Your company has one of the best management teams in the nation.
Assumption 3: The management team has responsibility for attracting new business.

ADVICE Don't let an accusation put you on the defensive. You may choose to accept, qualify, reject, or ignore any assumptions; however, if truth is on your side, you should find an opening to insert a message containing a positive theme. For example, you might emphasize current or anticipated capacity to attract business.

To win the audience's support or understanding, you may want to refer to the question as loaded. But be careful not to insult the questioner (unless the audience feels he is deserving). A smile or a humorous line such as "You've got me caught between a banana peel and a bear trap" might help.

Banana Peel 7—The Value Question

One of the first public arguments I can recall took place approximately 40 years ago in a grocery store in my hometown of Gardiner, Maine. Two of the patrons, both friends, got into a dispute over which ballclub was fielding a "better" team, the Boston Red Sox or the New York Yankees. The dispute escalated as each party tried to outperform the other in argument, command of baseball data, and ego. Yet neither had ever taken the time to reach an initial understanding regarding the criteria that would help them define "better."

Similarly, value questions can provoke controversy or confusion if the crucial terms are unclear.

EXAMPLE   Who was the better president, F.D.R. or Lincoln?

ADVICE

1. If the question per se and the audience are friendly, you might wish to ask them to define the vantage point they wish to apply to "better."
2. Alternatively, if you have a definition of "better" in mind, then you may wish to use it in your response with or without seeking the audience's approval.

Other Frequently Used Value Terms Often Requiring Definition

Competent/Incompetent	Good/Bad
Decent	Great
Effective/Ineffective	Impressive/Unimpressive
Excellent	Poor
Fair/Unfair	Strong/Weak

Banana Peel 8—The Multifaceted Question

Except for the hostile question, the multifaceted question is usually the most difficult to handle.

Why are multifaceted questions used? What factors make them particularly challenging to answer? And what tactical options does the executive have in responding to them? (Asked in one breath, this would be a multifaceted question.) And now for my answer(s).

We ask multifaceted questions for one or more of three reasons: to clear our agenda of questions, to pursue a line of logic reinforced by each facet, or, because we are unsure whether or not we will be called upon again; therefore, we're taking no chances.

Multifaceted questions can be particularly difficult to answer if: (1) there are three or more parts; (2) the phrasing of the collection becomes particularly long (increasing the burden of remembering them); (3) the elements of the question are not well related to one another; (4) the facets contain more than one type of banana peel; or (5) the facets vary in type from banana peels to a basic question of fact (see example below).

To make a multifaceted question more manageable for the respondent, you can announce that you have a two-, three-, or four-part question. This cue helps promote better listening, for without the cue, the facets tend to pile up by surprise.

The response options are illustrated below:

EXAMPLE "How many females do you employ? How has this level changed over the past four years? Why doesn't your firm's employment of females compare with that of competing firms? Why is there only one female on your board?"

ADVICE

1. If each facet can be remembered and answering all won't cause harm (assuming there is ample time), then answer fully.
2. On the other hand, if harm can be caused by answering a

remembered facet, it is probably best to "forget" it and answer the others.

3. Don't hesitate to ask for a facet to be repeated if you are reasonably certain you forgot a "safe" one.
4. If the questions cannot be realistically answered within the time alloted, politely say so.
5. Sometimes it may be advisable not to respond in the order in which the facets were asked. Journalists often insert a hostile "zinger" into the last facet, for example, "Doesn't all this prove that your management is dominated by male chauvinists?" In such instances, it is normally advisable to render the "zinger" impotent before answering the facets which preceded it.

I have seen many people have fun with the multifaceted question. One, a quick-witted, verbally facile banker, began his response with "First I'll answer your fourth question, then I'll answer your second and third, and then if I have time, I'll answer your first one."

Banana Peel 9—The Vague, Unfocused Question

"What is the meaning of life?" This classic question usually produces a paralyzing sense of puzzlement over how to respond. Another classic that frequently surfaces during a job interview is, "Would you mind telling me a little about yourself?" (Although it is technically a "Yes-No" question, if you want the job, you'd better elaborate.)

Vague, unfocused questions can liven up a philosophers' picnic. But they can also drive a detail-oriented person bonkers. Vagueness is rooted in two causes: the abstract nature of the concepts to be discussed, for example, "the meaning of life"; or the fuzziness of the phrasing, including word choice and syntax.

Sometimes vague questions are used to generate follow-up questions. A month ago I received a call from a political reporter I barely know who, knowing my active involvement on the national political scene, began our conversation with an unfocused "What's new?" I quickly seized the opportunity created by her question to explain the escalating importance of political debates (since we prepare candidates to appear in them).

The vague, unfocused question, although it can easily throw one off-stride, calls for only three straightforward response options:

EXAMPLE   "What are your company's plans for the future?"

ANALYSIS

1. Answer the question the way you wish—consistent with your substance and image goals.
2. Ask the questioner (if not hostile) to clarify.
3. Restate the question and respond in terms favorable to your persuasive goals.

Banana Peel 10—The "Yes-No" Question

The classic that immediately comes to mind when we think of the "Yes-No" question is *"Are you still beating your wife?"*

RESPONSE OPTION 1:
   "Yes"
AUDIENCE REACTION:
   "Oh, you still are."
RESPONSE OPTION 2:
   "No"
AUDIENCE REACTION:
   "Oh, at least you've stopped."

"Yes-No" questions can initially appear easy to answer, and many are (for example, "Have you eaten lunch yet?)." But they can also be extremely challenging, especially if loaded and leading (as in the example above). For example, try posing the following question to a presidential candidate, campaigning before a predominately white audience in the Deep South: "Yes or No: Would you have supported the observance of Martin Luther King's birthday as a national holiday?"

Three tactical options can reduce the likelihood that a "yes-no" question will make you one of the all-time squirmers.

EXAMPLE *"Interest rate fluctuations explain why your bank didn't do so well last year: Yes or no?"*

ADVICE

1. If "yes" or "no" is safe by itself, answer accordingly.
2. If risky, point out how the forced alternatives of "Yes" or "No" can interfere with a presentation of "the full truth." Then answer the question. Lines that can be helpful here are: "This can't be answered in simple 'yes-no' terms," "A 'Yes or No' would not do justice to your question," "This issue cannot be treated on a black-or-white basis."
3. You could also ignore the "Yes-No" framework and answer the question on your own terms, reinforcing your persuasive goals. For example: "Deregulation was an even more significant reason for our difficulty last year, but we've brought a few new products on stream that will make this year far more successful."

The amount of elaboration a response requires following a simple "yes" or "no" depends on two factors: first, who's doing the asking; second, the importance of the question to your persuasive goals. If the question is being asked by a superior or target-audience member who is undoubtedly looking for more than a "yes" or "no" headline, be obliging.

If the headline begins with a "yes" or "no," be careful. For example, if you were asked if you favored a controversial issue, for example, mandatory testing of employees for AIDS, and you immediately answered with a definitive "Yes" or "No," your response could have a polarizing effect on your audience, especially if an important segment disagrees with you. In such instances, you may be better served to highlight first the premises you share with your audience regarding the issue, and then to state your position, followed, if possible, by an alternate solution:

(If your answer is actually "No")

I realize that AIDS is a very serious problem—probably the most serious health problem our society has faced in our lifetimes. And I understand how it affects the workplace; it affects our sense of

security, personal relationships, and morale. However, testing of
employees is not the answer because. . . .

A final caveat regarding the "yes" or "no" question: Be
careful that you are not walking into a "gotcha" trap by
deliberately taking the phrasing of a "yes" or "no" question too
literally:

*REPORTER TO RELIGIOUS LEADER ACCUSED OF AN
IMPROPER FUNDRAISING SCHEME:*
"Isn't it true that you have established a commission system
for your fundraisers?

RELIGIOUS LEADER:
No.

REPORTER:
But I have evidence here that you have a point system for
fundraising whereby certain numbers of points entitle your
fundraisers to a wide range of prizes—all the way from
electric can openers to trips to the Orient.

RELIGIOUS LEADER:
We don't call it a commission; it's an incentive plan.

ANALYSIS:
Because the religious leader deliberately took the word
"commission" too literally and was not forthcoming in his
initial response regarding the "incentive plan," his evasiveness was not skillful, but transparent.

Knowing how to avoid "gotchas" requires considerable skill,
but when the dominant issue is credibility, playing cute can
create the perfect set-up for a "gotcha"—or a whole bushel of
them.

Banana Peel 11—The Either-Or Question

The Either-Or question is a close relative of the Yes-No question, for it implies only one of two choices.

EXAMPLE   "Why is the consumer advocate attacking you so
forcefully? Is it because of consumer pressure or because the
media has accused him of treating you with kid gloves?"

ADVICE

1. Do you feel that the consumer advocate is attacking you forcefully? If not, challenge the assumption.
2. You are being asked to speculate on the consumer advocate's motives—"to climb into his or her brain." Indicate that you can't speculate. If you say "ask the consumer advocate!" you may sound appropriately or inappropriately contentious. If a softer approach is preferred; an "I don't know" with a bridge to your positive message may be best.
3. With certain either-or questions (probably not this one) you may want to challenge one or both of the alternate premises (consumer pressure vs. media pressure) and provide a substitute for one or both premises—or provide more than two premises.
4. In so doing, you may wish to point out that the question is either-or, but the answer is not that simple.

Banana Peel 12—The Nonquestion

How often have you attended a speech at which an audience member stands up during the question-and-answer session and presents a statement or speech instead of a question? These circumstances are prompted by two main causes: the audience member was more interested in expressing an opinion or in ventilating emotions than in soliciting the speaker's opinion; or the questioner may not have noticed that although a question was intended, none was asked.

Nonquestions can be particularly tricky if they are potentially convincing accusatory editorials:

EXAMPLE (at an annual meeting) "You and your board have sold the shareholders down the river by approving a buy-out by a bank that is already in serious financial trouble."

ADVICE

1. Your composure must prevail. This includes your capacity to avoid going on the defensive and, as a possible result, inviting a potentially embarrassing debate.

2. Remember that too long a response can make you appear defensive.
3. Respond briefly and confidently to any claims or assumptions that may have won wide audience support, making sure to reinforce your persuasive goals.
4. In a nonhostile situation or when not dealing with a long-winded questioner, ask politely for the question. Asking admonishingly, "Well, what is your question?" can cause the audience to side with the questioner, unless they've already pegged him as a pain-in-the-anatomy.

QUALIFIERS

As helpful as the "banana peels" approach may be, it can be rendered virtually useless if any of your answers has a ring of certainty that is convincingly challenged by the questioner:

REPORTER DURING CRISIS INTERVIEW:
Are you sure that the skin of your aircrafts' fuselage was inspected recently?
AIRLINE EXECUTIVE:
Yes!
REPORTER:
Then why do the official inspection records indicate that the skin has not been examined for four years?

In this example—and in so many that come to mind—this executive should have monitored his tone of certainty and been prepared to use a qualifier to avoid the "banana peel." Some of the more frequently used qualifiers are "To the best of my recollection . . . ," "As far as I can determine . . . ," "Based on the information presented to me . . . ," and "According to the most reliable information. . . ."

There is, of course, a flip side to using qualifiers. Too many can damage your credibility by making you appear too cautious or unable to remember information key decision-makers, the media, or the public expect you to remember. Therefore, don't be surprised if a reporter or panelist at a legislative hearing asks pointedly, "What do you mean by 'to the best of my recollection'?" If this occurs, be prepared to explain nondefensively that you are committed to answering the questions as precisely and as responsibly as possible. Explain further that facts you may not be aware of could influence the full, unqualified truth behind your response.

A TIMELY ANECDOTE

The playwright Charles MacArthur, who had been brought to Hollywood to do a screenplay, was finding it difficult to write visual jokes. So he decided to turn to the comedic genius, Charlie Chaplin, for advice.*

CHAPLIN:

What's the problem?

MACARTHUR:

How, for example, could I make a fat lady, walking down Fifth Avenue, slip on a banana peel and still get a laugh? It's been done a million times. What's the best way to get the laugh? Do I show first the banana peel, then the fat lady approaching: then she slips? Or do I show the fat lady first, then the banana peel, and then she slips?

CHAPLIN:

Neither. You show the fat lady approaching; then you show the banana peel; then you show the fat lady and the banana peel together; then she steps over the banana peel and disappears down a manhole.

You are now prepared to deal with banana peels. However, I have no sage advice regarding the "manhole," unless it is a metaphor for what happens if your answers aren't truthful. If that is the case, perhaps the "manhole" metaphor is by itself a more striking message regarding the importance of truth than my pen could possibly capture.

---

* From the Little, Brown Book of Anecdotes, Little, Brown and Company, Boston, 1985.

CHAPTER 9

MANAGING HOSTILITY

Every April and May tens of thousands of America's shareholders make their traditional migration to an annual meeting. For many, the meeting provides an up-close look at management, including the opportunity to understand better the company's progress and plans for the future. For others, it can be good theater—especially if management comes under fire by vocal detractors reinforced by a responsive audience.

As good as the theater may be for the shareholder, these scenerios are no easy act for management. After all, in so many situations, management has worked diligently, resourcefully, and proudly to enhance shareholder value. Only a masochist would enjoy the verbal lashings that surround issues related to financial performance, size or nonpayment of dividend, executive compensation, and acquisitions.

The CEO holds no special claim to hostile audiences. Consider the schoolboard chairman who, in open meetings, regularly confronts outspoken parents and their views regarding controversial teachers, discipline, sex education, and censorship. Or the company engineer who has to convince citizens at a public hearing that the pipelines and exhaust stacks of her company's new chemical plant will not endanger the community.

How should you prepare for such encounters beyond anticipating the questions and thinking through the answers? The first piece of advice is to *value composure* (see Chapter 3). No better example of this comes to mind than the Reagan-Carter debate. As Reagan was preparing for the debate, the Carter camp had convinced a sizable segment of the American electorate that Reagan was too prone to push the nuclear button—

that he did not have the temperament to choose "more rational" approaches. To counter this image, we wanted the debate to showcase Reagan's reasonableness, advising him that "composure can speak as loudly—or more loudly—than content." Anyone who remembers the debate will recall that Reagan's composed, avuncular manner won the day and strengthened his margin of victory.

The most important advice I can give you in responding to hostility is to *depersonalize the hostility*—to separate your pride or ego as much as possible from your response and to concentrate as much as possible on your message, on the issues, and on your responsibility to yourself and to your organization.

Depersonalizing will help improve your ability to listen, including your opportunity to provide the detractor with an opportunity for cathartic relief, give you additional thinking time to develop an appropriate response, and prevent yourself from engaging in unnecessary debate that only weakens your impact and image.

As you face a hostile situation, ask yourself how well you understand the nature of the hostility being expressed. First, is "hostile" a fair term or is "anger," "frustration," "deep concern," or some other term more appropriate? Second, if "hostile" is the appropriate term, how widespread is the hostility? Remember, two or three (or more) hostile questioners do not automatically constitute a hostile audience. Remember also that an audience applauding a hostile questioner is not necessarily a hostile audience. They may merely agree with his message at the moment.

As you analyze more precisely the nature of the hostility, ask yourself these additional questions: Are you dealing with a person who is, by nature, hostile or are the circumstances creating or exacerbating the hostility? To what extent might the emotional content of the question or remark be more focused on the issue vs. you or your company? Or is the hostility mainly personal?

If you find that a sizable segment of your audience is hostile, a key question awaits you: To what extent are they part of your target audience—the people you want most to persuade? If the answer is "not significantly," then you have little to worry about as long as you maintain composure and project respect. If the answer is "significantly," then you are probably facing a tough uphill battle.

HOW TO CULTIVATE HOSTILITY

Wounds from uphill battles are frequently self-inflicted. Therefore, as you analyze the hostility expressed by one or more audience members, you should also analyze whether or not you may be inviting the hostility by being perceived as:

1. *Dishonest*. Once your credibility is in jeopardy, restoring it can be an uphill battle for the balance of your career.
2. *Inept*. Perceived competence is a major component of your credibility. Once confidence in your competence is seriously in doubt, it might be time to move on.
3. *Preventing reasonable access*. Not only does lack of access undermine internal morale, it can drive the media directly into a hostile mode.
4. *Evasive*. Again, a quality that your colleagues, your shareholders, nor the media can tolerate on a sustained basis.
5. *Selfish*. As soon as your boss, the board, the shareholders, or the media perceive your personal agenda to be taking precedence over the company's agenda, your potential for stardom immediately enters a holding pattern and invites hostility.
6. *Unfair*. Playing favorites, succumbing to selfish motives, acting in a heavy-handed or too-lenient manner can all generate hostility—very quickly.
7. *Improper*. As an executive you are expected to be a role model. Although occasional improprieties are normally tolerated, especially in the presence of prevailing positive qualities, perceived excess can generate a hostile climate.

Again, the key word is "perceived." And in every game of life, perceptions are realities.

PREEMPTING HOSTILITY

One way for you to prevent hostile questioning, or at least to soften it, is to preempt the more predictable hostile questions by answering them within the speech, presentation, or opening statement. This approach can help prevent you from being accused of deliberately avoiding the issue. In addition, your "preemptive strike" gives you better control both in the phrasing and tone of your remarks. Just as important, the "strike" can produce a framework for responding to hostile questions that may surface despite your preemptive efforts. However, for this approach to work, your preemptive rhetoric must be neither antagonistic nor unduly defensive.

Triangulation

What happens if you show undue disrespect toward a detractor? The diagram below will help answer this question.

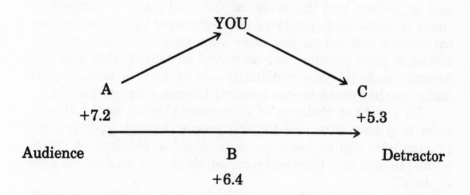

Arrow A indicates the audience's level of respect for you (10 being the highest). Arrow B indicates the audience's level of respect for the detractor and arrow C, yours for the detractor.

At any given point the numbers can change. If, for instance, you say something to the detractor that the audience regards as highly inappropriate, your level of respect (line A) may drop and the detractor's (line B) may increase. The key message of this example is that although the audience's respect for you may be higher than that for the detractor, they do respect him and, when appropriate, will react to reinforce that respect.

Tactical Options

Persuasive Bonding
In addressing a hostile audience, particularly if they are part of your target audience, seek out areas of perceived commonality. Can you build upon the trustworthiness component of your credibility by referring to a shared experience, attitude, value, or goal? Is there a way you can win their trust without appearing phony or manipulative?

Let's consider this scenario: You are a Ph.D. psychologist representing a leading manufacturer of videogames. A study just released by a major university concludes that videogames promote aggressiveness and other forms of antisocial behavior. You are invited to appear on a national talk show with one of the researchers who conducted the study. She's smooth, attractive, and articulate, and the evidence she presents is so compelling that the studio audience is quickly influenced by her. As you are introduced and before you utter your very first word, you, by virtue of your position, are perceived as biased. How can you attempt to build your credibility—to at least neutralize this audience that could at any moment become outright hostile?

Do you have children of videogame-playing age? Can you refer to a long career of helping people through your private practice? Do you or have you specialized in children of video-game-playing age (currently called child and adolescent psychology)?

If you answer "no" to any of these questions, the audience's aggressiveness toward you might pale in comparison to that ostensibly spawned by videogames. If you answer "yes," you might have a fighting chance.

The Appeal for a Fair Hearing
Many speakers I've worked with enter a room knowing that the audience was "loaded for bear"—so loaded that interruptions and heckling made it virtually impossible to speak. What should you do if this happens to you?

If the chair of the meeting (if there is one) can't secure you a fair hearing, then you may need to make the appeal on your own. As you do, remember that few people are willing to admit that they do not believe in fair play and freedom of speech. Therefore, as you make your appeal, be aware of what you are trying to accomplish psychologically: you are attempting to diminish the conflict between you and your audience by emphasizing the higher-minded bonding (common ground) you share with them over fair play and freedom of speech.

A possible approach:

> Please, please. You invited me here (appeal to proper hospitality). I know that we may have differences of opinion, but all I ask for is a fair hearing—just fairness on your part in the true democratic fashion—so that both sides can be heard. In return, I promise to be as to-the-point as possible.

The Format and the Hostile Questioner

When you have control over the format, you have added control over the hostile questioner as well as the monopolizer. The annual shareholders' meeting is a perfect example. The many options appropriate for this setting—and selectively appropriate for other large forums—include:

1. Inviting questions only from those entitled to speak, for example, shareholders, registered voters, dues paying members, etc.
2. Asking that each person identify himself by name. This tack makes the questioner accountable vs. anonymous.
3. Requesting that only one question be posed at a time.
4. Requesting questions only—not statements. If you decide to exercise this option, try not to sound too heavy-handed.
5. Requesting conciseness or placing a time limit on the question. A 1-, 2-, or 3-minute limit is more likely to be tolerated when more than 150 to 200 people are present and a high level of participation is expected.
6. Requesting that each questioner move to a microphone or wait for an usher to move the microphone to him to ask questions. This helps prevent a hostile questioner or monopolizer from jumping up and down to ask

> questions and forces him to wait his turn if others are
> anxious to speak.
> 7. Asking that the person sit down and be quiet. This is
> appropriate if reasonable attempts have been made to
> address the person's concern and he is clearly attempt-
> ing to disrupt the meeting.
> 8. Ordering that the person's microphone be turned off if
> the situation gets out of control.
> 9. Ordering security to remove the person. This is a *last,
> last* resort, which must be preceded by one or two
> warnings.
> 10. Calling a recess or adjourning the meeting. These are
> very last resorts; they should be exercised only when
> the entire meeting appears out of control.

Eye Contact

As you begin to respond to a hostile questioner, do look directly
at him. Generally, you should not feel obliged to look at him
throughout your entire response; doing so could force you into
taking one or more follow-up questions. Therefore, try to make a
point within your response that allows you to turn your body,
head, and eyes to another audience member, preferably one not
seated too closely to the hostile questioner—and preferably a
member of your target audience.

The Private Meeting

As annual meetings approach, it is not unusual for the chairman
of a corporation or his designee to meet in advance with a
shareholder known to be hostile. The private meeting not only
accords the shareholder a measure of respect, it allows him to
vent his concerns while the executive attempts to address them.
Regardless of whether or not the meeting produces constructive
understanding, the executive emerges from it better prepared to
anticipate the hostile shareholder's questions, including the
importance he attaches to them.

The private meeting is also a useful approach when facing a
hostile questioner who rises to express a personal complaint that
requires fact-finding by you or by someone designated by you.
This approach has, for instance, worked well with electric utility

speaker's bureau members who regularly address consumer groups and receive complaints about billing procedures. The key to making this approach work well for you is to have the right line ready, for example, "Since your question is more of a personal nature, let's discuss it personally at the end of the meeting."

Demonstrating Understanding of and Respect for the Opposing Position

Hostility can be diminished by the audience's perception that the speaker understands and respects their point of view. In such instances it may be advisable to verbalize the audience's position clearly and respectfully within your prepared remarks and answers, and then explain why you both differ with it.

HOSTILE QUESTIONER:

Who needs this industrial park in the first place?

CHAMBER OF COMMERCE OFFICIAL:

It seems clear to me that the reasons why you don't want the industrial park in your area is your concern for how it will affect traffic patterns, contribute to noise and air pollution, and undermine the residential status of your neighborhoods. Allow me to respond to your concerns and to raise some additional points.

ANALYSIS A clear and tactful demonstration of understanding. However, be careful not to raise negative points about your proposal that the audience may not be considering. Otherwise, you may be "poisoning your own well."

Concern/Compassion/Empathy

Although this subject was developed earlier (Chapter 3), it deserves special mention here because the expression of concern, compassion, or empathy can signal genuine understanding of the hostile questioner's concern and, in some instances, be all that he expects:

CEO TO A SENIOR CITIZEN SHAREHOLDER:

I'm sorry to hear how our financial performance has affected your income.

UTILITY EXECUTIVE TO A CUSTOMER:

> I understand the frustration you've faced in trying to straighten out your bill and I will. . . .

CONGRESSMAN DURING A "TOWN MEETING":

> *(to a senior citizen whose Social Security check got lost in the mail)* I realize how important that check is to you and I will. . . .

The "Yes-But" Technique

As you listen carefully to a hostile questioner, ask yourself whether or not you can agree with any of his statements or assumptions before taking your own position. This can neutralize the hostility and build common ground and credibility between you, him, and the portion of the audience identified with him.

CHAMBER OF COMMERCE OFFICIAL:

> *(at a public meeting)* I completely agree with you that traffic in this area has become too congested. I also agree with you that new development has a lot to do with it. But I ask you to suspend judgment regarding your 'no more new development' position until the town fathers decide whether or not a more sophisticated development plan than the one we relied on in the past could work for our community.

Monitoring the Burden of Proof

A hostile questioner stands up in a meeting conducted by you and fires a "shotgun blast"—a fusillade of unsubstantiated accusations against your actions, motives, and character. In addition to following the advice already presented, how do you handle this situation?

- Avoid going too far on the defensive. You are under no obligation to defend yourself against unsubstantiated charges. *Remember:* Technically, the burden of proof is on the accuser, although you should not normally invite him to uphold it; otherwise, you might be relinquishing control by allowing him to strengthen his case against you.

- Keep your target audience in mind and respond to the claims that may have influenced them the most as you consider ignoring or giving less attention to the other claims.
- Consider the persuasive value of forceful, flat denial, recognizing that a more elaborate response can make you appear defensive.

HOSTILE SHAREHOLDER:

The only reason Ruszenas is on your board is because when he was Mayor he gave your firm a lot of business.

YOU:

Your statement is completely unfounded and irresponsible.

Note: A tone of righteous indignation (as opposed to outright anger) may be appropriate in situations like these.

- Decide whether or not the turning-the-tables tactic will be effective in these situations. George Bush chose this tactic for Dan Rather during the 1988 presidential race when Rather badgered him regarding his role in Reagan's arms-for-hostages scheme.

RATHER:

Mr. Vice President, you've made us hypocrites in the face of the world. How could you, how could you sign on to such a policy?

BUSH:

(*a few moments later*) It's not fair to judge my whole career by a rehash on Iran. How would you like it if I judged your career by the 7 minutes when you walked off the set (in anger) in New York? How would you like that?

Initially, Bush's play was regarded as a masterstroke that helped him diminish the "wimp" image that had been plaguing him for months—if not years. In addition, it symbolically put the media in its place. But after less than a week had passed, people shifted from a focus on the cleverness of the tactic to a more serious examination of Bush's role in the Iran-Contra affair.

Humor

The use of put-down humor can be effective in hostile situations, especially if the audience does not identify strongly with the questioner, but does identify well with the respondent.

QUESTIONER:

> All you care about is profits, profits, and profits. You drive big cars, eat at the fanciest restaurants, take nice vacations, and wear the nicest clothes. When are you going to show more concern for the little guy?

RESPONDENT:

> I'm only 5′4″ myself. And by the way, I like your silk tie.

In some situations this respondent would have had his audience in stitches; in others, he would be courting disaster. In essence, good humorists are good risk-assessors.

CHAPTER 10

COMBATTING SILENCE

One day a communications officer from a large corporation called me to discuss a problem that surfaced during their past management meeting: once the senior officers had delivered their speeches, few of the several hundred officers and managers seated in the audience rose to ask a question. Their silence was deafening, for a major goal of the meeting was to facilitate two-way communication.

Why do situations like this occur—and, I might add, why so frequently?

THE FORMAT

Turn first to the meeting format. Is it so laden with speeches, despite allocated time for Q & A, that the audience's spirit to participate is dampened? I am quite accustomed to seeing a program filled with 40- to 50-minute presentations followed by a 10- to 20-minute Q & A session. But in many instances, the time allocations for remarks and Q & A should be reversed. Give a speaker 45 minutes and chances are he'll use it up, regardless of whether or not he needs it. In fact, most 45- to 50-minute presentations given to me before a major meeting should be trimmed by 30 to 50%. This is especially true if the major goal of the presentation is to establish and reinforce a theme rather than educate.

You do have an alternative (which I discussed in a different context in Chapter 6). If you insist that you need 40 or more minutes consider dividing your presentation into segments. For example, you may choose to stop your presentation for Q & A after 10 to 25 minutes and at the end.

This approach has several advantages: it allows the audience to feel more involved; it provides you with feedback regarding your presentation; and it gives you a better sense of your audience as you continue the presentation. The only disadvantage is that it requires you to be a skillful moderator during each Q & A segment, and particularly, to know when and how to return to your presentation.

Another format option (selected by the firm that contacted me) is to shrink the size of the original audience by scheduling a series of smaller breakout sessions following the remarks. These sessions should be more facilitative for two reasons: first, they are devoted exclusively to Q & A; second, they provide a more intimate and informal environment where the questioner feels less exposed to so many people.

MANAGEMENT'S TONE

Another major reason why the audience may be reluctant to participate is the tone of management's remarks. Although an executive may want his presentation to spur discussion or even controversy, the tone of the content and delivery is either one-way or *fait accompli*. Despite the executive's request for questions or feedback at the end, the inadvertent nonverbal message he transmits is "We really don't need your input; this is a take it or leave it proposition."

Such a situation involves what communication researchers call "conflicting communication." Specifically a "conflict" exists between the verbal message ("We want your feedback") and the nonverbal tone ("We don't . . ."). According to the research, we tend to place much more credence on the nonverbal message than on the verbal one.

Projecting a More Facilitative Tone

What specifically can management do to make sure that the Q & A session doesn't turn to dead silence?

If management is sincere in its desire to facilitate Q & A,

then it should consider laying out the Q & A agenda within the presentation itself. For example:

I'll discuss with you now some new ideas we're thinking about to improve the efficiency of our distribution system. We're *not sure* how well they *might work* or *whether they will work at all.* So I will look forward to your feedback on these ideas during the Q & A.

ANALYSIS Note the tentative tone highlighted by the italics. The ideas do not have the ring of *fait accompli,* and the speaker's request for feedback sounds genuine.

Once the presentation has been made, you have additional options to make the Q & A more conducive to two-way communication.

1. To project a more approachable image, you can come out in front of the lectern, lean on it, sit on the edge of a table, or walk into the audience. To complement this image, a man may remove his jacket, loosen his tie, and roll up his sleeves. A woman's options are more limited. But, whatever options you choose, be careful not to come across as too manipulative.

2. Verbally, you may need to break the ice with a line that genuinely invites participation: "The purpose of this conference is to promote two-way communication and we really need your feedback" or "Every question is a good question."

3. In the same vein, whenever possible, learn and use the questioner's name (without sounding forced or patronizing). This can make the communication more personal and less contentious.

4. Avoid transmitting unduly negative feedback to comments and questions, recognizing that this feedback can be communicated both verbally and nonverbally (e.g., a dismissive tone). Instead, find ways to convey positive feedback without sounding patronizing.

   Unduly Negative Feedback: "I can't agree with that at all," "What makes you think that?" (*in a challenging tone*), and "That's ridiculous."

   Positive Feedback: "That's a very helpful suggestion," "Perhaps we *should* give more thought to your idea," or "I'm not sure that we looked at it that way."

5. It is best that you decide beforehand how much you wish to engage the audience verbally—how much give and take you want—beyond simply answering their questions. As effective as the give-and-take may be, a commitment to it requires that you be prepared to monitor your tone even more carefully. The risk of being too argumentative, autocratic, or both normally increases in proportion to the length of the exchange.

6. If you genuinely want to know what is on your managers' minds, consider the value of questioning over asserting. By questioning, you are demonstrating interest in their point of view. By asserting, you are seeking to inform or persuade, not to learn.

7. Put your quality listening traits on full display. Cutting one of your managers off midstream can be the kiss of death. Not only will it offend him, but the other managers may be offended as well (see Triangulation, page 139).

8. Don't take yourself too seriously. Be prepared to indicate lack of knowledge ("I didn't know that"), admit fault ("I really screwed that one up"), and display tentativeness ("I'm not quite sure how we should proceed"). Self-deprecating humor—as well as humor in general—can also be effective:

   Heavy person late for a Q & A session: "I'm sorry I'm late, but when the waitress placed the dessert tray next to my table I didn't know until I paid the check that it wasn't all mine."

9. Be willing to display a certain amount of openness by referring to feelings or personal experiences, including shared experiences. This helps your audience sense your trust in them and helps build their trust in you. Put another way, the more closed you are, the less approachable and facilitative you will be.

10. Be prepared to demonstrate concern, compassion, or empathy in a genuine manner.

AUDIENCE RELUCTANCE

No matter how approachable and facilitative management's tone may be, two audience factors can impede a lively Q & A session: speech fright and the fear of embarrassment.

Speech fright certainly doesn't end at the edge of the stage. Questioners can experience it as well, particularly in large group settings which can stimulate a paralyzing sense of self-consciousness. This feeling can be exacerbated if the person has to stand, identify himself (shedding the security of anonymity), and walk to a microphone placed in the aisle.

The fear of embarrassment can be just as strong an impediment—or even stronger. Since managers are understandably conscious of their job security and opportunity for advancement, they do not want to pose a question that sounds "stupid," angers the superior, or comes off as showing off or "kissing up." Hence they choose silence.

Back-Up Tactics

Although you plan to do everything to make your address and Q & A session as participative as possible, you must be prepared to deal with "the terrible silence" if it occurs. These tactics could prove helpful:

"Talking to Yourself"

You complete your remarks, receive polite applause, invite questions in a friendly, positive manner, and then enter the zone of deadly silence. This can be handled with normal discomfort, but without fluster, by saying to your audience: "While you are thinking about what questions to ask, let me raise and answer a few that are frequently asked by our managers."

"The Survey Says"

To break the ice, consider asking your audience questions. Begin with easy closed-ended, survey-type questions such as, "How many of you have seen the videotape on our new distribution network?" Then slowly begin to solicit attitudes: "How many of you think the network will help?" "Why?"

"The Invisible Plant"
This approach can be especially effective if the questions do not appear to be planted. There are two ways to prevent this: first, make the question challenging (remembering that challenging questions generally bring out the best in us); second, don't read the question.

The *"Harding Hopper"*
President Warren G. Harding conducted his press conferences by requiring reporters to submit questions in advance. He then assembled the press corps, selected the questions he wanted to answer, and while they watched, tossed the others into a wastebasket. Imagine the media and public outcry if this approach were attempted by a President today.

However, this approach has survived in business and professional meetings where the speaker or program chairman removes from a container questions prepared in advance. Often the questions are prescreened to prevent duplication and to ensure clarity. Although this approach may encourage persons reluctant to ask questions to place one in the hopper, it is hardly conducive to an open, natural, spontaneous, two-way flow of communication—especially if the questioner's name is not disclosed.

Mingling
You've tried everything and the Q & A session is nevertheless bombing. Your one remaining option is to invite the audience to ask their questions as you mingle with them following your remarks.

PART V

PREPARATION PLANS AND PRACTICE

Q & A mastery requires more than a solid grasp of the concepts presented so far—and more than the finely tuned ability to put them into practice. It also requires a comprehensive, systematic, control-oriented approach to prepare for both questioning and responding—an approach that contrasts sharply with the "wing-it" mentality that is all too often doomed to mediocrity or failure.

This part provides preparation plans and special advice for the following types of Q & A:

The Q & A Session Following a Speech or Presentation
The One-on-One Print, TV, or Radio Interview
The News Conference
The TV or Radio Talk Show
The Job Interview
Testifying at a Legislative or Government Agency Hearing

Once your preparation plan has been followed, you will need to practice. The section "Practice, Practice, Practice" (p. 196) is filled with practical insights that should help make your dry runs, and ultimately your actual performance, successful.

PREPARATION PLAN

THE Q & A SESSION
FOLLOWING A SPEECH
OR PRESENTATION

The Q & A session following your speech or presentation is a prime opportunity to advance your persuasive goals, whether you are promoting an idea, product, or service. Therefore, instead of letting your guard down following your remarks, be ready to persuade further, especially since the Q & A session allows you to address the issues that interest your target audience the most. To be ready, prepare for the session carefully, relying on the preceding chapters, and on the following preparation plan.

GOALS AND OPPORTUNITIES

1. Rank order which of the following statements represent your two or three major goals for the Q & A session:
   - _____ a. To provide informed/credible answers supportive of your overall position/presentation.
   - _____ b. To represent the corporation's or organization's views as its key decision-makers would want them expressed.
   - _____ c. To encourage the purchase of your product or service.
   - _____ d. To discern the audience's views regarding the issues at hand.

_____ *e.* To provide the audience with the sense that you support two-way communication with them.

_____ *f.* To diffuse the audience's concerns.

_____ *g.* To facilitate and maintain control of the discussion.

_____ *h.* To avoid gaffes, misstatements, or volunteering too much. (*circle your particular concern*)

_____ *i.* Other.

2. Do you regard the Q & A session mainly as an opportunity or as an obligation? Why?

   ADVICE Don't participate in the session until you have a positive attitude regarding how it can help you accomplish both your substance and image goals.

KEY MESSAGES AND TARGET AUDIENCE

1. What key messages do you intend to reinforce during your Q & A session?

   ADVICE Normally, you should not have more than three or four key messages. Place them on a piece of paper you can refer to during the Q & A.

   a. What is their relative order of importance?

   b. What proof or support can you provide for each key message?

   c. What visual aids do you need to support your key messages?
   (1) Photographs or real exhibits
   (2) 35 mm projector
   (3) Overhead projector
   (4) Flip chart
   (5) Other

   ADVICE

   1. Make sure you can access the visual quickly.
   2. Don't forget the spare bulb, pointer, and marking pens.

3. Place transparencies (also called foils or overheads) in cardboard frames for easier handling.

2. Using the scale below, how would you rate your target audience's regard for each of the following channels of persuasion:

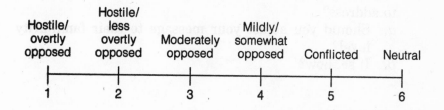

Hostile/ overtly opposed	Hostile/ less overtly opposed	Moderately opposed	Mildly/ somewhat opposed	Conflicted	Neutral
1	2	3	4	5	6

Mildly/ Somewhat supportive	Moderately supportive	Strongly but less overtly supportive	Actively supportive
7	8	9	10

_____ *a.* You

_____ *b.* Your corporation

_____ *c.* The company or division of the corporation you represent

_____ *d.* Your industry, business, profession

_____ *e.* Your principal message

3. Why do you think they react to each channel in the manner you have indicated?

4. How would you describe your target audience?

    a. How relevant are the following factors?

        (1) Age

        (2) Sex

        (3) Socioeconomic status

        (4) Education

        (5) Religion

        (6) Race

        (7) Whether or not they are parents

        (8) Whether or not they live in a certain area

        (9) Other

    b. How do you intend to incorporate the more relevant factors into your message?

    ADVICE If the stakes are high and your audience is small, for example, under 25, you should attempt to focus your analysis on each audience member.

5. What is their level of familiarity with the issues you plan to address?
       a. Should you adjust your message to their familiarity level?
       b. If so, how?

IMAGE GOALS

1. What major image goals do you wish to achieve as a result of the Q & A session?
       a. What image traits should you consciously avoid? (e.g., defensiveness, aloofness, anger, condescension, etc.)
       b. How specifically do you intend to achieve your image goals through:
           (1) The responses per se?
           (2) Your demeanor?

THE AUDIENCE'S GOALS

Rank order your audience's two or three principal goals.
    _____ *a.* To achieve information
    _____ *b.* To be inspired or entertained
    _____ *c.* To demonstrate support for you personally or for your point of view
    _____ *d.* To take pleasure in seeing you in person (especially if you are a celebrity)
    _____ *e.* To secure an opportunity to meet you and develop a personal relationship with you
    _____ *f.* To experience cathartic relief through questioning

      _____ *g.* To exploit your appearance as a forum for expressing a contrary point of view

      _____ *h.* To embarrass you

      _____ *i.* To destroy the meeting

      _____ *j.* Other

FORMAT AND NORMS

1. Will other speakers be on the program?
   a. Who?
   b. What will be their order of appearance?
   c. What will they speak on?
   d. What is the audience's regard for them according to the above scale?
2. Who will moderate the Q & A session and how?
   a. How will the questions be delegated to a speaker for a response (for a panel or symposium)?
   b. How long is the session expected to last?
   c. How will it be introduced and ended? By the moderator or host or by you?
   d. Should you be prepared to identify any topics as off-limits?
   e. What signal system should you have with your host for extending or ending the session?
   f. Is some type of reception planned following the Q & A? How long will it last?
3. Will you be sitting or standing for the Q & A?
   ADVICE Most persons I advise prefer standing when this option seems appropriate, noting that it gives them a greater sense of command or control.

4. If standing is your preference, where should you stand?
   a. Does a lectern reinforce or undermine your image goals?
   b. If you leave the lectern, will you need a special microphone?
   c. Will you be well illuminated?

ADVICE If you wish to appear engaging or approachable, leaving the lectern is probably advisable, unless doing so will place you in the dark or cause you to upstage another speaker.

5. What are the dimensions and layout of the room, including the seating arrangement?
   a. Can you be assured that there will be no noise penetration from the adjoining room?
   b. Will audience members address you from their seats or come to an aisle microphone?
   c. Will they have name tags or tent cards you can read from your position? Or should you ask them to identify themselves and their affiliation?

   ADVICE Referring to them by name (without sounding patronizing) can make the interaction more personable and the questioner more accountable. That is, the anonymous questioner is generally less accountable.

6. Will the media be present?
   a. Who?
   b. Will they participate in the questioning?
   c. Will they want to interview you separately?

   ADVICE The media will sometimes want to interview you before you have an opportunity to mingle with your audience. If mingling is more important, you may wish to ask the media to wait or arrange for the interview later.

7. Will or should any parties be deliberately excluded from the session? Why?
8. What approaches are you prepared to take in case you run into a hostile audience member or audience?
9. What approaches are you prepared to take if your audience is silent?
10. If you plan a team presentation, have you decided who will respond to which lines of questioning? Are you prepared to explain why you are handing the "ball" off to a colleague?
11. Do you intend to practice your individual or team presentation? If so, when and how?

PREPARATION PLAN

THE ONE-ON-ONE PRINT, TV, OR RADIO INTERVIEW

Media interviews, even for the media savvy, are frequently a source of concern. When we are interviewed we often wonder or worry whether the interview will turn out fair, positive, accurate, and focused on our key messages. The reporter also has concerns. He or she wants the interview to be truthful, candid, and interesting, and can feel frustrated when one of these qualities is missing. Whether you are the interviewee or the reporter, this preparation guide should help you reduce your concerns and meet your goals.

THE INTERVIEWEE

GOALS AND OPPORTUNITIES

1. Rank order which of the following statements represent your two or three major goals for the interview. *Note:* If you are the reporter, rank order the two or three goals you regard as uppermost in the interviewee's mind.
   - _____ *a.* To generate a favorable story
   - _____ *b.* To control the interview
   - _____ *c.* To represent the corporation's or organizations's views as the company's key-decision-makers would want them expressed
   - _____ *d.* To advance a particular point of view regarding an issue or story

_____ *e.* To elevate the interviewee's personal exposure

_____ *f.* To elevate the corporation's or organization's exposure

_____ *g.* To avoid gaffes or other types of blunders

_____ *h.* To avoid unnecessary disclosures

_____ *i.* To avoid/generate controversy/confrontation (circle choice)

_____ *j.* To develop a productive relationship with the reporter

_____ *k.* Other

2. As the interviewee, do you regard the interview mainly as an opportunity or as an obligation? Why?

ADVICE Do not give the interview until you clearly define its potential benefits.

KEY MESSAGES AND TARGET AUDIENCE

1. What key messages do you intend to convey and reinforce during the interview?

    ADVICE For seated print and radio interviews, your key messages can appear on a sheet in front of you. Just be sure that the purpose of the sheet is not too obvious to the reporter.

    a. What is the relative order of importance of your key messages?

    b. What proof or support can you provide for each key message?

2. How would you describe your target audience?

    a. What demographic and knowledge level factors of your target and general audiences are most relevant to each key message?

    (1) Age

    (2) Sex

    (3) Socioeconomic status

    (4) Education

    (5) Religion

   (6)   Race
   (7)   Political preferences
   (8)   Whether or not they are customers
   (9)   Whether or not they are parents
   (10) Whether or not they live in a certain area
   (11) Other
   b. How do you intend to incorporate the more relevant factors into your message?
3. Using the scale below, how would you rate your target audience's regard for each of the following channels of persuasion:

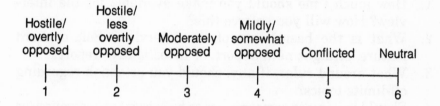

Hostile/ overtly opposed	Hostile/ less overtly opposed	Moderately opposed	Mildly/ somewhat opposed	Conflicted	Neutral
1	2	3	4	5	6

Mildly/ somewhat supportive	Moderately supportive	Strongly but less overtly supportive	Actively supportive
7	8	9	10

   _____ a. You
   _____ b. Your corporation
   _____ c. The company or division of the corporation you represent
   _____ d. Your industry, business, or profession
   _____ e. Your principal message
4. Why do you think they react to each channel in the manner you have indicated?
5. What is their level of familiarity with the issues you plan to address?
   a. Should you adjust your message to their familiarity level?
   b. If so, how?

IMAGE GOALS

What major image goals do you plan to achieve as a result of the interview?

1. What image traits should you consciously avoid?
2. How do you intend to achieve your image goals through:
   a. Your responses?
   b. Your demeanor?

NORMS

1. How much time should you make available for the interview? How will you enforce this?
2. What is the basic slant of the interview? Soft or hard feature, straight news report, or investigative report?
3. What ground rules, if any, should you establish regarding off-limits topics?
4. Should you invite someone else to be present as a resource or witness?
5. Should you tape-record the interview?
6. Where should the interview take place?
7. To what extent do you want to control the setting, for example, remove confidential items, place items you wish to discuss within easy view, make the environment neater than usual, etc.?
8. To what extent will you agree to speaking "off-the-record," "not for attribution," or on "background?" (See the Inside Advice Section.)

SPECIAL PREPARATION

1. How much do you know about the reporter?
   a. Have you been interviewed by him or her before? What was your experience?

   ADVICE Don't assume that your experience will be similar from one interview to the next.

    b. What is his or her general reputation for competence and fairness?

    c. What is his or her interest, knowledge level, and attitude(s) regarding your company and industry?

    d. What is his or her interview style? (friendly, aggressive)

2. If you need to learn more about the reporter, what sources are available to you?

    a. Clippings or videotapes

    b. Colleagues who know the reporter or his or her reputation

    c. Published ratings

3. How much do you know about the channel, station, or publication?

    a. How credible is it?

    b. Is it identified with a particular slant?

    c. How have you or your firm dealt with it before?

4. When is the reporter's deadline?

5. Should you make background materials/exhibits available?

6. If the reporter is interviewing you as part of an ongoing story, what has been its drift? Who has spoken? What have they said?

7. What lines of questioning and specific questions (including banana groves and banana peels) should you expect?

    a. Are you fully prepared?

    b. If not, what steps should you take to make sure that you are?

8. What type of access should you provide to the reporter following the interview?

INSIDE ADVICE FOR THE INTERVIEWEE

1. Since a live interview cannot be edited, you have more potential control over content than with a taped interview.

2. When consenting to an interview, request the topics to be covered. In fact, if the interview is expected to be friendly, you may even want to ask for questons in advance. But be ready to be turned down.

3. There is no such thing as a dead microphone or tape recorder and the camera is "always" on.

4. Beware of the "pregnant pause" in which the radio or TV reporter holds the microphone in front of you after you've finished your response, hoping you will extend your answer and possibly place you closer to a banana peel. If this occurs, look the reporter in the eye with a confident, friendly smile (not grin) and wait for the next question.

5. The interview is not over until you and the reporter have gone your separate ways.

6. If you don't want to be quoted in a print interview directly and want to cooperate, you may comment if the reporter agrees that your remarks be treated according to one of the following three provisions:

   a. *On Background.* Here you will not be referred to by name. Instead you might be referred to as "a company source," or as a "reliable source close to the situation."

   b. *On Deep Background.* This proviso implies an understanding between you and the reporter that every effort will be taken not to imply or to allow the inference that you are the source. This can be particularly restrictive to the reporter—so much so that information given "on deep background" may not be usable.

   c. *Off-the-Record.* This means that the information presented is not to be linked to you in any way. I do not believe in "off-the-record" remarks, although this proviso remains a matter of continuing controversy among communication professionals.

      In choosing any of these three options, make sure that you and the reporter share the same understanding of each option, including clarity regarding when each begins and ends.

7. Avoid saying "no comment," especially on TV or radio; otherwise, this expression can taint you with the perception of guilt. If you choose not to comment, be prepared to explain why in a nondefensive manner.

8. Shorter answers are normally more advisable than longer ones. Whenever possible, analyze the actual news program to determine how long the responses tend to be rather than rely on a general principle that your answers should be no

longer than "x" seconds. Remember, if the reporter wants more information, he or she will ask for it.

9. Know how to end the interview. Ask your secretary or public information officer to determine—or negotiate—when the interview is arranged how long it should take. Reinforce the agreed upon time (and any other ground rules) right before the interview begins. Arrange for your secretary to signal you shortly before the interview is scheduled to end.

THE REPORTER/INTERVIEWER

GOALS AND OPPORTUNITIES

1. Rank order the following based on how well they represent your two or three major goals for the interview. *Note:* If you are the interviewee, rank order the two or three goals you regard as uppermost in his or her mind:

   _____ *a.* To ascertain facts
   _____ *b.* To secure a statement
   _____ *c.* To advance a point of view with the viewers, listeners, or readers
   _____ *d.* To bring about some specific form of social change
   _____ *e.* To serve as a surrogate of the people
   _____ *f.* To secure through this story an opportunity for advancement or for a journalism prize
   _____ *g.* To elevate exposure of self, station, network, or affiliate
   _____ *h.* To develop a future source relationship
   _____ *i.* Other

IMAGE GOALS

What major image goals do you intend to convey and avoid?

1. What major image traits do you intend to avoid?
2. How do you intend to achieve your image goals through:
   a. Your questions?
   b. Your demeanor?

SPECIAL PREPARATION

1. How much do you know about the interviewee and his or her company and industry or profession?
2. Should you learn more before the interview? How?
3. What issues do you need to probe during the interview?
   a. What questions should you ask to probe them?
   b. How should they be phrased and sequenced?
4. How much time do you need?
5. What interview setting is most advantageous for accomplishing your goals?
6. When is your deadline?
7. Should you tape record the interview?

PREPARATION PLAN

THE NEWS CONFERENCE

The news conference—especially a crisis conference—may place you in a lion's den where reporters will seem to compete aggressively to exact from you every available pound of flesh. Your ability to survive the conference—*and to succeed in it*—requires control, credibility, and composure. This guide will assist you in meeting these challenges.

GOALS AND OPPORTUNITIES

1. Rank order which of the following statements represent your two or three major reasons for calling the news conference.
   - _____ *a.* To make a positive announcement
   - _____ *b.* To respond to a negative story or crisis situation
   - _____ *c.* To offer a single consistent message
   - _____ *d.* To secure maximum media exposure
   - _____ *e.* To limit the number of one-on-one media interviews
   - _____ *f.* Other

2. How confident are you that the conference is advisable?
3. Has its advisability been sufficiently discussed?

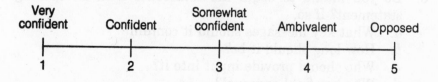

Very confident	Confident	Somewhat confident	Ambivalent	Opposed
1	2	3	4	5

THE SPOKESPERSON

1. Why has this spokesperson been chosen? Is he or she the best person to face the media?
2. Has your company or organization taken sufficient steps to control who is permitted to speak to the media?
3. Rank order which of the following statements represent the spokesperson's major goals:
   _____ *a.* To generate a positive story
   _____ *b.* To demonstrate corporate credibility
   _____ *c.* To represent the corporation's or organization's views as its key decision-makers would want them expressed
   _____ *d.* To control the interview
   _____ *e.* To avoid gaffes and other types of blunders
   _____ *f.* To avoid unnecessary disclosures
   _____ *g.* Other

3. As the spokesperson, do you regard the interview mainly as an opportunity or as an obligation?
   ADVICE Even in a crisis situation, you should be focused primarily on using the conference to convey positive substance and image messages regarding your company or organization.
4. If this is a crisis situation, are you currently perceived more as the victim or as the culprit?
   a. If you are perceived as the victim, could this perception change to your being perceived as the culprit? If so, how?
   b. If you are perceived as the culprit, how fair is this perception? If unfair, to what extent can you reverse it?
5. Are other people available to provide technical support for your remarks?
   a. How prepared are they to face the media?
   b. How prepared are they to reinforce your key messages?
6. Do you intend to begin the conference with an opening statement? If so,
   a. What key messages should it contain?
   b. How long should it be?
   c. Who should provide input into it?
   d. Who has final approval?

ADVICE Generally, an opening statement (usually no longer than 5 minutes) is advisable to lay out your key messages and to provide a framework for responding to the more predictable crucial questions. If should be practiced separately from the Q & A dry run to reflect the desired tone or image. In addition, it should be distributed to the media, often with a news release.

KEY MESSAGES AND YOUR TARGET AUDIENCE

1. What key messages do you intend to convey and reinforce during the news conference?
   ADVICE Keep a key message sheet in front of you making sure that the purpose of the sheet is not too obvious to the reporters.

   a. What is the relative order of importance of your key messages?
   b. What proof or support can you provide for each key message?
2. How would you describe your target audience—those people beyond the confines of the briefing room whom you need to influence?
   a. How relevant are the following factors?
      (1) Age
      (2) Sex
      (3) Socioeconomic status
      (4) Education
      (5) Religion
      (6) Race
      (7) Political preferences
      (8) Whether or not they are customers
      (9) Whether or not they are parents
      (10) Whether or not they live in a certain area
      (11) Other
   b. How do you intend to incorporate the more relevant factors into your message?

3. What is their level of familiarity with each of the issues you plan to address?
    a. Should you adjust your message to their familiarity level?
    b. If so, how?
4. Using the scale below, how would you rate your audience's regard for each of the following channels of persuasion:

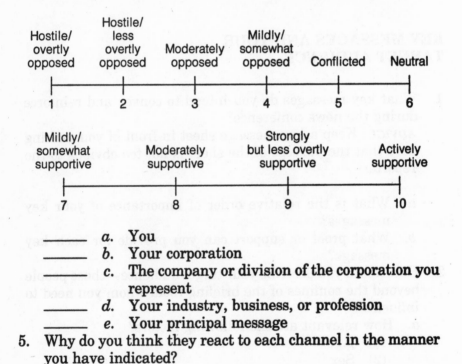

_____ a. You
_____ b. Your corporation
_____ c. The company or division of the corporation you represent
_____ d. Your industry, business, or profession
_____ e. Your principal message
5. Why do you think they react to each channel in the manner you have indicated?

IMAGE GOALS

What major image goals do you plan to achieve as a result of the conference?

1. What image traits should you consciously avoid?
2. How do you intend to achieve your image goals through:
    a. The opening statement and your responses?
    b. Your demeanor?

ADVICE In a crisis conference, you must be particularly wary of projecting defensiveness, undue anger, loss of control, and loss of composure. If the conference is called to report on a matter involving injury, loss of life, or a health hazard, or to make a negative employment-related announcement, for example, to announce a major layoff or plant closing, then it is generally advisable to express compassion early in the opening statement and to reinforce it during the Q & A.

FORMAT AND NORMS

1. Where should the conference be held? Why?
   ADVICE Make sure you have a lectern, enough seating, and adequate lighting. Also, the room should be available for camera crews to set up 30 to 40 minutes before the conference begins. Light refreshments may be advisable.

2. When should it take place?
   ADVICE Normally, news conferences occur at approximately 10 A.M. to take advantage of the daily news cycle. However, in a crisis situation, a news conference can be called at any time—even several times—throughout the day.

3. How should you announce the conference?
   a. By telephone?
   b. By news release?
   ADVICE Choose whichever method seems most efficient. In fact, both methods occasionally work well in tandem. You should normally announce the topic in advance. This allows news editors to decide which reporters to send and whether or not camera crews should accompany them.

4. Who should introduce you and end the conference?
   a. What kind of signal system should the introducer have with you that the conference should end?

ADVICE Usually news conferences should end when the questioning is beginning to die out or sound too repetitious—or if the climate is deteriorating into seemingly irreversible hostility.

b. Should the introducer signal you if you are overanswering the question?

ADVICE Using a "third base coach" to signal you is probably advisable if you tend to overanswer.

5. What topics should be prohibited (e.g., for legal reasons, or when facts are not yet available) and why?

6. Who should be permitted (and not be permitted) to attend? How will attendance be reinforced?

7. Should you ask reporters to identify themselves by name and affiliation?

ADVICE If you don't know most of the reporters, this may be advisable to allow you to identify which ones can most likely reach your target audience.

8. Should you tape record or videotape the conference?

ADVICE Whenever possible you should. Doing so gives you a verification record of what you said and a fine opportunity for analyzing your performance.

9. Should you allow a tour of the facility or scene of the crisis?

ADVICE This decision should be weighed very carefully. As soon as photographers and camera crews take pictures of a crisis which developed on your premises, they increase the likelihood that the story will reflect negatively on your company or organization. Therefore your verbal refusal may be less negative than the graphic potency of the pictures taken or video taping made during the tour.

SPECIAL PREPARATION

1. How much to you know about the reporters who are expected to attend?

    a. Have you been interviewed by any of them before? What is your experience with them?

    b. What is the general reputation of each major reporter for competence and fairness?

    c. What are the major reporters' interests, knowledge level, and attitudes regarding your company, the industry, and the issue at hand?

    d. What do you know about the interviewing style of each?

2. If you need to learn more about a reporter, what sources are available to you?

    a. Clippings or videotapes

    b. Colleagues who know the reporter or his or her reputation

    c. Published ratings

3. How much do you know about the channel, station, or publication?

    a. How credible is it?

    b. Is it identified with a particular slant?

    c. Have you or your firm dealt with it before?

4. If you are being interviewed as part of an ongoing story, what has been its drift? Who has spoken? What has been said?

5. What questions (including banana groves and banana peels) should you expect?

    a. Are you fully prepared?

    b. If not, what steps should you take to make sure that you are?

PREPARATION PLAN

THE TV OR RADIO TALK SHOW

Don't let the comfortable living-room atmosphere of a talk show set deceive you into thinking that a talk show is any less formidable than most interview settings. Depending on the host, the format and, of course, you and your subject, even the most ostensibly benign talk show can quickly become brutalizing. Whether you are a guest or the host, the key to performing well on talk shows is to understand them well, especially since, as this guide illustrates, preparation often involves great attention to detail.

THE INTERVIEWEE

GOALS AND OPPORTUNITIES

1. Rank order which of the following represent your two or three major goals for the show. *Note:* If you are the talk show host, rank order the two or three goals you regard as uppermost in the guest's mind:
   - _____ *a.* To advance a particular point of view regarding an issue or story
   - _____ *b.* To represent the corporation's or organization's views as its key decision-makers would want them expressed
   - _____ *c.* To encourage the purchase of your product or service
   - _____ *d.* To elevate the interviewee's personal exposure

——— *e.* To elevate the corporation's or organization's exposure

——— *f.* To avoid gaffes, misstatements, or volunteering too much (*circle your particular concern*)

——— *g.* To avoid/generate controversy/confrontation (*circle choice*)

——— *h.* Other

2. As the interviewee, do you regard the interview mainly as an opportunity or as an obligation? Why?

   ADVICE Don't appear on the show until you have a positive attitude regarding what you can potentially accomplish.

KEY MESSAGES AND YOUR TARGET AUDIENCE

1. What key messages do you intend to convey and reinforce during the show?

   ADVICE For a radio talk show, you may choose to place your key messages on a sheet of paper in front of you. Be sure that the purpose of the sheet is not too obvious to the host, especially if the circumstances are not friendly.

   a. What is the relative order of importance of your key messages?

   b. What proof or support can you provide for each key message?

2. How would you describe your target audience?

   a. How relevant are the following factors?

      (1) Age

      (2) Sex

      (3) Socioeconomic status

      (4) Education

      (5) Religion

      (6) Race

      (7) Political preference

      (8) Whether or not they are customers

      (9) Whether or not they are parents

      (10)   Whether or not they live in a certain area
      (11)   Other

   b. What factors are most relevant to each key message?

   c. How do you intend to incorporate the more relevant factors into your message?

3. What is the audience's familiarity level with each of the issues you plan to address?

   a. Should you adjust your message to their familiarity level?

   b. If so, how?

4. Using the scale below, how would you rate your target audience's regard for each of the following channels of persuasion:

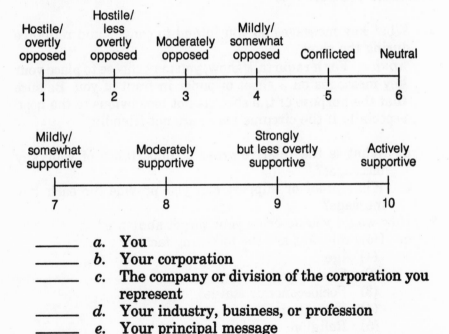

  _____ *a.* You

  _____ *b.* Your corporation

  _____ *c.* The company or division of the corporation you represent

  _____ *d.* Your industry, business, or profession

  _____ *e.* Your principal message

5. Why do you think they react to each channel in the manner you have indicated?

IMAGE GOALS

What major image goals do you wish to achieve as a result of the interview?

1. What image traits should you consciously avoid?
2. How do you intend to achieve your image goals through:
    a. The content of your comments and answers.
    b. Your demeanor.

FORMAT

1. What is the length of the show?
2. Will it be live or taped? If taped, when will it be shown?
3. How large a segment of your target audience is expected to watch it?

    ADVICE   In certain circumstances, you may wish to encourage viewership via internal announcements, Mailgrams, and so forth.

4. Are other guests expected to appear?
    a. Who will they be?
        (1) Will their message be related to yours?
        (2) If so, will this require special preparation?
    b. How will they appear?
        (1) Live with you?
        (2) On a split screen from a "remote" location?
        (3) By voice only via telephone?
    c. When will they appear, before or after you? How will this influence your presentation?

    ADVICE   If, for instance, your adversaries will be appearing after you, it may be wise for you to preempt them by refuting their point of view.

5. Will the show include:
    a. A live audience questioning segment?
    b. A call-in segment?

6. If the answer to *a* or *b* or both is yes:
   a. When will the segment occur?
   b. How long will it last?
   c. What lines of audience questioning can be expected?
   ADVICE   Often live audiences for talk shows are selected based on interest in a specific topic. In fact, sometimes interest groups successfully "stack" talk-show audiences and call-in segments with informed, articulate advocates. Don't hesitate to ask the producer for background information regarding how the live audience is selected.

7. How do you expect to be introduced?
   a. By the host saying to the camera, "Our guest today is . . . ?"
   b. By an off-camera announcer introducing you?
   c. During interaction with the host, which includes a "welcome to the show"?
   d. By the host firing a "zinger" at you to throw you immediately on the defensive?
   ADVICE   If the introduction is friendly, be prepared to nod and smile as soon as you are introduced. Otherwise, the audience may sense that you are detached. Also, be prepared to respond with a "nice to be here, *host's first name.*" If you're hit by a zinger, be prepared to respond forcefully to the claim *without attacking the host*.

8. What is the seating arrangement in relation to the overall set design, including the location of cameras?
   ADVICE   Secure a diagram in advance. Sometimes you can choose where to sit when more than one guest is appearing at the same time. If you regard your appearance as more of an opportunity than as a risk, you may wish to sit closest to the host. This is usually the "power seat" for two reasons: the camera can capture you most easily; and your presence and body language can engage the host more easily than those of the guest seated three chairs away.

THE HOST

1. What is the host's general reputation and the reputation of the show?
2. What is the host's questioning style?
    a. Mild-mannered?
    b. Aggressive?
    c. Hostile?
    d. A combination of the above?
    e. Other?
3. To what extent does the host take/suggest a stand?
4. How much control does the host exercise over the interaction?
    a. Significant?
    b. Moderate?
    c. Varied?
    d. Little?
5. To what extent does the host:
    a. Allow guests to complete responses?
    b. Provide fair rebuttal opportunities?
    c. Control interruptions?
    d. Control monopolizers?
6. What specific questions or lines of questioning can you expect?
7. What types of banana groves and banana peels are the host likely to rely on?
8. What other tactics does the host use?
    a. Shaking head in disbelief.
    b. Asking the audience "do you believe that?"
    c. Hurling accusations at guests.
    d. Using the cliff-hanger zinger right before a commercial break.

ADVICE The preceding eight questions can be best addressed by watching and analyzing one or more shows before you appear. Avoiding surprises is an important prerequisite to achieving talk-show mastery.

SPECIAL ADVICE

1. Be prepared to avoid distractions on the set (technicians moving around, cameras, etc.) by focusing squarely on the host or on the person talking. Do not look into the camera unless you are addressing a call-in viewer.
2. Generally, you should not debate the host. Remember, even if members of your target audience may be listening, their loyalty to the host may be stronger than their loyalty to you.
3. Don't refuse make-up if it's offered and one of your key advisors considers it necessary.
4. When sitting, assume a comfortable position, but be prepared to demonstrate energy, involvement, and conviction by leaning forward and gesturing, and through facial expression and vocal emphasis.
5. Be prepared to compete to be heard. The show may require an atypical amount of aggressiveness—not aggression—by you.

THE HOST

GOALS

1. Rank order which of the following represent your two or three major goals for the show. If you are the guest, rank order the two or three goals you regard as uppermost in the host's mind:
   _____ *a.* To ascertain facts
   _____ *b.* To help the audience achieve greater understanding
   _____ *c.* To generate a news item
   _____ *d.* To advance a particular point of view regarding an issue or story
   _____ *e.* To generate conflict or controversy
   _____ *f.* To bring out the "true personality" of the guest
   _____ *g.* To ask "good" questions
   _____ *h.* To "control the flow" well

_____ *i.* To represent the show, station, network, or self
favorably (*circle most important choice*)
_____ *j.* To serve as a surrogate of the people
_____ *k.* Other

PREPARATION

1. How much do you know about the guest and his or her company and industry or profession?
2. Should you learn more before the interview? How?
3. What issues do you need to probe?
   a. What questions should you ask to probe them?
   b. How?
4. What specific image goals should you achieve during the show? What image traits should you avoid? How do you intend to achieve them?
5. If you are expecting a very special guest for an exclusive interview, should you practice?

PREPARATION PLAN

THE JOB INTERVIEW

Employment interviews are usually high-stakes interactions for both interviewee and interviewer. When they are, both parties should abandon any temptation to "wing it," for doing so can result in poor answers, weak questions, and, just as important, the omission of crucial questions. This guide provides a practical skeletal framework for preparing for most any employement interview.

THE INTERVIEWEE

GOALS

Rank order which of the following represent your two or three major goals for the interview. *Note:* If you are one of the interviewers, rank order the two or three goals you regard as uppermost in the interviewee's mind.

_____ *a.* To convince those interviewing you that you deserve an offer

_____ *b.* To determine whether or not the position is a match for your skills and talents

_____ *c.* To determine whether or not you and your possible new boss and colleagues have the right "chemistry" with one another

_____ *d.* To learn about advancement opportunities

_____ *e.* To learn about salary and benefits

_____ *f.* Other

KEY MESSAGES AND YOUR TARGET AUDIENCE

1. What key messages do you intend to convey during the interview?
   a. What is their relative order of importance?
   b. What proof or support can you provide for each key message?
2. How would you describe your target audience (the key sources of recommendations and decision-makers)?
   a. What demographic factors of your target audience are most relevant to each key message?
      (1) Age
      (2) Sex
      (3) Socioeconomic status
      (4) Religion
      (5) Race
      (6) Degrees received
      (7) Persons known in company
      (8) Special interests
      (9) Schools attended
      (10) Other

   b. How do you intend to incorporate the more relevant factors into your message? For example, if you and the interviewer attended the same school or majored in the same subject, you may choose to mention this to build common ground. But be careful not to sound too obvious. Forced common ground can cause you to lose ground.

IMAGE GOALS

1. What major image goals do you plan to achieve as a result of the interview?
   a. What image traits should you consciously avoid?
   b. How do you intend to achieve your image goals through:
      (1) The message itself?
      (2) Your demeanor?

FORMAT AND NORMS

1. Where will the interview take place?
2. Will it be a single interview or will it progress during the day (or on several different days) in stages?
   a. If in stages, what will they be?
   b. Who are the key people involved in the various stages?
3. Will any formal testing be required? If so, what will it be?

SPECIAL PREPARATION

1. Have you done everything reasonably possible to learn about the company, its principals, the position, and the industry? For example, have you consulted:
   a. The annual report
   b. The Moody and Standard and Poors profiles
   c. A financial analyst's report (which can be gotten from a broker)
   d. Informed colleagues, friends, and acquaintances
   e. The *New York Times Index, Business Periodicals Index,* and other major reference sources
2. What lines of questioning and specific questions do you expect?
3. Are you thoroughly familiar with your resume and its relevance to the position for which you are applying?
4. Does your resume have any inherent banana peels, for example chronological employment gaps, frequent job changes, incomplete undergraduate or graduate training, etc.? Can you respond honestly and credibly to these?
5. What specific questions should you ask during the interview?
   a. How important is each?
   b. When should each be asked?
6. Should you be specially prepared for any formal testing?
7. Should you role play the interview before participating in it?

THE INTERVIEWER

GOALS

Rank order which of the following represent your two or three major goals for the interview. *Note:* If you are one of the interviewees, rank order the two or three goals you regard as uppermost in the interviewer's mind.

_____   *a.*   To determine if the interviewee is a good match for the position

_____   *b.*   To assess the interviewee's compatibility with potential colleagues

_____   *c.*   To convince the interviewer to select your firm

_____   *d.*   To learn about how the interviewee's current or former employer handles certain situations

_____   *e.*   To get a general feel for the quality of the people available for the position

_____   *f.*   To allow the interviewee to convince you that the position for which he or she is applying is necessary

_____   *g.*   Other

KEY AUDIENCE/DEMOGRAPHICS

ADVICE   For legal and ethical reasons, these criteria are not applicable here. Each interviewee should be evaluated solely on perceived ability.

APPROACH

1. How much time should you allocate for the interview?
2. Where should you conduct it? Why?
3. Where are your key messages?
    a.   What is their relative order of importance?
    b.   What proof or support can you provide for each one?

4. What are your image goals?
   a. What image traits should you consciously avoid?
   b. How do you intend to achieve your image goals?
5. What lines of questioning and specific questions should you pursue?
6. Are you sufficiently familiar with the applicant's resume?
7. Have you thoroughly checked his or her references by asking the "right" questions?
8. How well can you describe the position being offered?
9. Should you introduce the applicant to your colleagues?
10. How much hospitality should you extend? One or more meals? A tour? A company orientation film?

PREPARATION PLAN

TESTIFYING AT A LEGISLATIVE OR GOVERNMENT AGENCY HEARING

There was probably a day when you regarded testifying before a legislative committee or regulatory agency as very remote from your professional responsibilities. However, today you may consider testifying as an important opportunity to exercise control over the destiny of your product, service, or cause. In fact, testifying—especially on a voluntary basis—may be a sign of status and influence. The same is true for serving as a panelist on such committee. To make your appearance work for you, think carefully about the questions and advice contained in this guide.

THE WITNESS

GOALS AND OPPORTUNITIES

1. Rank order which of the following represent your two or three major goals for the hearing. *Note:* If you are one of the questioners, rank order the two or three goals you regard as uppermost in the witness' mind.
   - _____ *a.* To advance a position or a cause (*offensive strategy*)
   - _____ *b.* To get through the hearing with minimal damage (*defensive strategy*)

_____ *c.* To support/oppose legislation or regulatory approval (*circle the appropriate choices*)

_____ *d.* To defend or promote one's reputation

_____ *e.* To advance one's career, for example, to secure speaking engagements, job offers, book/movie contracts, legal defense fund donations, etc.

_____ *f.* To obtain strong media coverage

_____ *g.* To elevate the exposure of a company or organization

_____ *h.* To protect confidentiality/secrecy

_____ *i.* To avoid gaffes and other types of blunders

_____ *j.* Other

2. Do you regard the hearing as more of an opportunity or as an obligation? Why?

   ADVICE Don't testify until you clearly perceive the opportunity that testifying presents.

3. How important is the hearing to the ultimate legislative or regulatory decision or recommendation to be made by the panel?

   _____ *a.* Extremely important

   _____ *b.* Very important

   _____ *c.* Somewhat important

   _____ *d.* Not important

   Why?

KEY MESSAGES AND TARGET AUDIENCE

1. What key messages do you intend to convey and reinforce during the hearing?

   a. What is the relative order of importance of your key messages?

   b. What proof or support can you provide for each key message?

2. Is your target audience:

   _____ *a.* The panel?

   _____ *b.* The media?

      ———   *c.* Your constituency?

      ———   *d.* A combination?

Why?

3. How would you describe your target audience(s)?

    a. What demographic and knowledge level factors of your target and general audiences are most relevant to each key message?

        (1) Age

        (2) Sex

        (3) Socioeconomic status

        (4) Education

        (5) Religion

        (6) Race

        (7) Whether or not they are parents

        (8) Whether they live in a certain area

        (9) Other

    b. How do you intend to incorporate the more relevant factors into your message?

4. What is your target audience's familiarity level with each of the issues you plan to address?

    a. Should you adjust your message to their familiarity level?

    b. If so, how?

5. Using the scale below, how would you rate your target audience's regard for each of the following channels of persuasion:

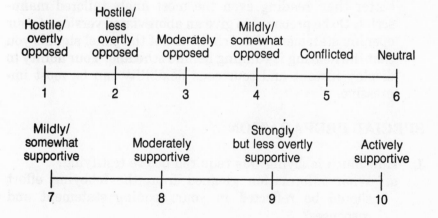

_____ *a.* You
_____ *b.* Your corporation
_____ *c.* The company or division of the corporation you
represent
_____ *d.* Your industry, business, or profession
_____ *e.* Your principal message
6. Why do you think they react to each channel in the manner
you have indicated?
7. Where specifically does each panelist stand regarding your
proposal? Why?

IMAGE GOALS

What major image goals do you wish to achieve as a result of the
hearing?
  a. What image traits should you consciously avoid?
  b. How do you intend to achieve your image goals through:
  (1) Your opening statement and responses
  (2) Your demeanor

> *ADVICE* Generally, it is far more advisable to *communicate*
> with the panel by presenting your opening statement
> extemporaneously than by reading it. (Your written
> statement can nonetheless be submitted for the record.) The
> extemporaneous approach allows you to develop a more
> direct interaction with the panel—one which conveys the
> force of your personality, including your conviction—far
> better than reading even the most finely tailored manu-
> script. Do be prepared to give an abbreviated version of your
> opening statement if the chairman of the panel signals you
> that the hearing is running behind schedule. Your ability to
> display instant and courteous flexibility can be most im-
> pressive.

SPECIAL PREPARATION

1. How much lobbying was required before testifying?
  a. What information gleaned from the lobbying effort
  should be reflected in your opening statement and
  responses?

   b. What questions (including banana groves and banana peels) can you expect—and from whom?
2. To what extent should the testimony of the other supportive witnesses be coordinated?
3. What can you learn in advance about the hearing demeanor of each panelist including the chair?
   a. Aggressiveness in questioning style
   b. Skill as a questioner
   c. Tendency to use the hearing as a soapbox
   d. Compliance with the ground rules
   e. Relationship with the other panelists
   f. Other
4. Are large exhibits (e.g., charts, enlarged photographs) allowed and advisable?
5. Should you be accompanied by your spouse or another prominent supporter? (Remember the stoic, supportive presence of John Dean's wife, Maureen, during the Watergate hearings.)
6. What is the overall layout of the room, including specific seating arrangements? If possible, visit the room well before you testify.

THE PANELIST

GOALS

1. Rank order which of the following represent your two or three major goals for the hearing. *Note:* If you are one of the witnesses, rank order the two or three goals you regard as uppermost in the panelists' minds.
   _____ a. To discover the facts required to resolve the issues at hand
   _____ b. To advance/defend an issue or a cause
   _____ c. To support/prevent legislation or regulatory approval
   _____ d. To secure strong media coverage
   _____ e. To promote or defend one's reputation
   _____ f. To enhance the profile and reputation of the panel
   _____ g. To build up the witness and his or her testi-

mony, or to cast doubt on the testimony (*circle the appropriate choice*)

_____ *h.* Other

INSIDE ADVICE ON CROSS-EXAMINATION

Since legislative and regulatory hearings are often dominated by lawyers, it is not unusual for them to put their cross-examination skills on full display—especially if the media are present. The following advice, although directed to the questioner, can give the respondent added insight into the questioner's tactics:

1. Keep your questions clear, concise, and close-ended to control the communication—and their pressure on the witness.
2. Take full advantage of silence—especially following a dramatic admission.
3. Focus mainly on the crucial issues.
4. Don't ask a crucial question until the foundation for it has been firmly laid.
5. Avoid conveying the impression that your emotions rule your reason.
6. When your point is made, stop!*

FORMAT AND NORMS: A CHECKLIST FOR PANELIST AND WITNESS

1. Will the hearing be open or closed?
2. What will be the length of the hearing?
3. What other supportive and adversarial witnesses are expected to appear?
   a. When and in what order?

_____

*The classic advice "ask only questions to which you already know the answer" is controversial. See: Charles W. Smith, Sr., "Cross-Examination: Use of the 'Cover Question.'" *Trial Diplomacy Journal*, Winter 1982/83, pp. 25–28.

b. Will their appearance, including the order, influence your message? If so, how?
4. What is the expected attendance pattern of the panelists?
5. How strongly does the chair exercise his or her leadership authority? Under what particular circumstances?
6. Do you expect a supportive panelist to speak out on behalf of your position or to attempt to "rescue you" if another panelist treats you unfairly?
7. Will an attorney be present? If so, what will be his or her role?
8. What specific ground rules apply regarding who is permitted to ask questions, prior submissions, the opening statement, the process of questioning, the opportunity to be called back to testify?
9. Do immunity provisions for witnesses apply?
10. Will time limits be placed on opening statements and questioning?
11. Do opening statements have to be read or can they be delivered extemporaneously?

PRACTICE, PRACTICE, PRACTICE

Whether you are preparing for a high-stakes presentation, annual meeting, media interview, crisis news conference, legal or legislative hearing, or job interview, I can't emphasize the importance of practice enough.

People who resist practice sessions usually voice one of these four objections (followed by my abbreviated response):

OBJECTION 1

How will I find the time?

RESPONSE

This is a priority; you have no choice!

OBJECTION 2

I'm good with Q & A.

RESPONSE

Perhaps you are, but in this situation you need to be "extra-good"—you need to be sharp!

OBJECTION 3

I'm more comfortable in the Q & A session than in the presentation.

RESPONSE

Comfort is not the issue; the issue is **maximum credibility and** persuasive impact!

OBJECTION 4

A practice session will make me uptight—too self-conscious.

RESPONSE

Not if it is planned and executed well—with your input.

PLANNING AND EXECUTING THE PRACTICE SESSION

A productive practice session requires careful planning based on the following criteria that will serve as the basis for this discussion: The format should be tailored to the respondent's comfort level and learning style. For high stakes engagements, the environment should simulate as much as reasonably possible the circumstances of the actual event. Key resource persons should be available to provide feedback.

The Format

When John Kennedy prepared for his first debate against Richard Nixon in 1960, he was lying in bed, reading the questions prepared on index cards, responding, and then tossing them aside. When Jimmy Carter and Ronald Reagan prepared for their debate with one another 20 years later, each practiced in a fully outfitted, mock television studio with a stand-in playing his opponent.

The difference between Kennedy's approach and Carter's and Reagan's is not so related to sophistication over time as to the temperament of each man and how he wanted to prepare.

In choosing a format, you need to understand what aspects of it work or don't work well for you. The following questions and advice place this issue in perspective:

QUESTION *When do you want the session to take place?*

ADVICE Whenever possible, the first practice session should take place sooner rather than later. This provides more time to reflect on your strategic approach and prevents any last-minute panic that can undermine your performance.

Whether or not you practice the day of your performance is up to you. Sometimes, especially in crisis situations, you have no choice. When you do have a choice, a few warm-up questions on the day of your engagement can be helpful.

QUESTION   *How long do you want the session to last?*

ADVICE They generally take longer than one expects—usually 2 to 6 hours.

QUESTION   *Should you discuss goals, key messages, and strategy before you begin to field questions?*

ADVICE Usually you should.

QUESTION   *Do you want to receive feedback following each response? Or do you prefer to cover a round of questions first?*

ADVICE Feedback following each response is usually a more thorough approach, but is less time-efficient than conducting it following each round.

QUESTION   *Do you want to videotape your responses and then analyze them via replay on an individual response or round basis?*

ADVICE Although a full replay on either basis is often desirable, when pressed for time, replay the more important responses, especially the ones that gave you the most difficulty.

QUESTION   *As you analyze your responses for content, do you want immediate feedback regarding strategy and style—or do you prefer that later?*

ADVICE Normally it is best to provide it following each response, but after the content has been resolved. Ronald

Reagan, in preparing for his debate with Jimmy Carter, preferred feedback following each round, starting with substance and moving to strategy and style (my role). Although the sessions were videotaped, because of time pressures, we did not engage in replay.

QUESTION *Do you want to engage in self-analysis before inviting feedback from others?*

ADVICE By doing so, you will set the tone for your receptiveness to criticism and can preempt feedback you'd rather not hear first from others.

QUESTION *Should you identify the criteria to be used during the feedback session, for example, clarity, responsiveness, credibility, persuasiveness, appropriate length, etc.?*

ADVICE This is often a good idea.

QUESTION *Should you be taking notes during the feedback session, or should someone else do this for you?*

ADVICE Entirely a personal decision.

QUESTION *Should a transcript of the practice session be made for more in-depth analysis?*

ADVICE This can be very helpful, not only to identify weaknesses, but also to capture in writing responses and phrases that were especially effective.

The Environment

Most of the annual meetings, major news conferences, talk shows, and debates for which I have prepared executives and candidates have involved full simulations with television cameras and lights, the exact lectern to be used during the engagement, the same type of chair, the identical room layout, etc. Yes, these simulations can be time-consuming and expensive, but especially in high-stakes situations, they are ususally worth it for two major reasons: first, they can help you alleviate the fear of the unknown; that is, a quality simulation is tantamount to a full dress-rehearsal in which details are addressed and the element of surprise is significantly preempted. Second, the simulation often imposes a sense of focus and discipline over the practice session, qualities that may not be as obvious during more informal sessions.

Whenever possible, a full simulation should be preceded or followed by a visit to the actual site of the engagement. In fact, some simulations can take place at the actual site, for example, an internal board or committee meeting, an annual meeting, or a news conference.

The Resource Team

Too many people in the practice session quickly calls up the "too many chefs can spoil the broth" analogy. A chorus of discordant views reinforced by well-meaning but unduly harsh critics can result in a reliable recipe for instant disaster.

To prevent disaster and make the team work for you, consider the following advice: Invite only those persons who are likely to contribute constructively. When in doubt, "don't mail the invitation." Consider giving each team member "homework" in advance, for example, preparing questions or issue positions. This prevents them from taking a "wing-it" approach to the session and increases your chances that the more significant questions will be asked. Encourage them to meet separately in advance to review questions and proposed answers. This can help prevent unnecessary overlap as well as time-wasting—and potentially confusing—conflict. Make sure your team knows the ground rules before the practice session begins—including who is in charge.

Do Questioners Rehearse?

Absolutely. Consider this *Time* magazine account of Dan Rather's preparation for his cause célèbre interview with George Bush before the 1988 Iowa caucuses:

> The day of the interview Rather had three one-hour rehearsals with six people involved in the broadcast. He was coached as if he

was a candidate preparing for a debate or a pugilist preparing for a fight, rather than a journalist going into an interview. Howard Rosenberg, a producer from CBS's Washington bureau, played Bush. "We knew it was going to be a brawl," said (Richard) Cohen (senior political producer of the Evening News).

Although Rather was wise to rehearse, the one thing missing from his rehearsal was the counterattack question posed by Bush. In sum, Rather didn't rehearse enough.

POST-PERFORMANCE FEEDBACK

Notice that I didn't title this discussion "post mortem." As you know, this term means "after death," hardly an appropriate way to describe your performance if you faithfully followed my advice.

Whatever term you prefer, any important performance should be followed by a feedback session that captures many of the essential features of the practice session. This session can be especially valuable if a videotape or audiotape was made of your performance. It can be even more valuable if a verbatim transcription is also available.

Don't conduct the feedback session until your defenses are down and your dispositon toward self-improvement is high. And when you do, remember that your constructive critics may need feedback from you to indicate your receptiveness to their feedback.

EPILOGUE

THE ETHICS OF Q & A

The English poet and critic, Alexander Pope, once said, "He who tells a lie is not sensible how great a task he undertakes, for he must be forced to invent twenty more to maintain that one."

Wise and timeless advice for sure. Yet pressures facing today's executives can often blur the distinction between truth and falsehood. When push comes to shove, can a white lie told by an executive to an audience, reporter, or government panel help preserve the corporation's image and his or her own career path? Possibly, but the risks are, as Pope stated, entirely too great.

In reviewing our ethical standards as communicators, we must draw a clear line between truthfulness and openness. Truthfulness means that whatever we say is, to the very best of our knowledge, factual and free from distortion. Openness implies the extent to which the faucet of factual and interpretive information should be opened. Therefore, as communicators, we should be absolutely truthful, while our openness should be relative or situational.

In establishing a personal set of standards for ethical communication, we should adhere to the following advice:

- Be secure enough to say "I don't know" rather than feign knowledge—and possibly expose your charade unwittingly—thereby compromising your credibility.
- Combat any tendency to distort a reality through the selective use of language, examples, numbers, or statistics.
- Scrutinize your logic for any tendency to engage in fallacious reasoning.

- Double or triple check your sources for accuracy, proper context, reputation, and recency.
- Check the methodology behind any studies on which your case depends.
- Avoid any temptation to fabricate examples or other data when your case seems deficient.
- Be prepared to acknowledge persons who deserve credit for the good ideas or expressions you are using.

When setting our standards for ethical communication, we can derive added insight and guidance from the well-chosen words of William Penn: "Truth often suffers more by the heat of its defenders than from the arguments of its opposers."

SELECTED BIBLIOGRAPHY

Brown, Peter Megargee: *The Art of Questioning, Thirty Maxims of Cross-Examination*, New York, Macmillan Publishing Company, 1987.

Drake, John D.: *Effective Interviewing, A Guide for Managers*, New York, Amacom, 1982, 1972.

Ehrlich, J.W.: *The Lost Art of Cross-Examination, or Perjury Anyone?*, New York, Dorset Press, 1987.

Irvine, Robert B.: *When You Are the Headline: Managing a Major News Story*, Illinois, Dow Jones-Irwin, 1987.

Leeds, Dorothy: *Smart Questions: A New Strategy for Successful Managers*, New York, McGraw-Hill, 1987.

Martel, Myles: *Political Campaign Debates: Images, Strategies, and Tactics*, New York, Longman, Inc., 1983.

Molloy, John T.: *The New Dress for Success*, New York, Warner Books, 1988.

ABOUT THE AUTHOR

Myles Martel, Ph.D., president of Martel & Associates (Villanova, Pennsylvania), is one of America's premier executive communication consultants. He has advised and trained hundreds of the nation's corporate and political leaders (including 26 United States Senators) for speeches, presentations, and media appearances. He achieved national prominence in 1980 by serving as Ronald Reagan's personal debate advisor.

    Dr. Martel has appeared on numerous radio and TV programs, including *ABC Nightly News* and *Nightline with Ted Koppel*. His work has been featured in several national publications, including the *Wall Street Journal, Harpers,* and *U.S. News & World Report*. He is the author of two other books: *Before You Say a Word* and *Political Campaign Debates: Images, Strategies and Tactics*. He received his Ph.D. and M.A. in Speech Communication from Temple University and his B.A. from the University of Connecticut. He resides in Radnor, Pennsylvania, with his wife and son.

CONTRIBUTORS

The following people provided consulting opportunities and, in many instances, concepts and examples reflected in this book. Their cooperation is appreciated:

Griffin Allen
Rick Anthony
Sharyn Arnold
John Baldwin
Patricia Barron
Sue Benheim
Norm Blanchard
Joaquin Bowman
Jim Brenneman
Vince Breglio
Al Butkus
George Butler
Jim Cavanaugh
Rob Cawthorn
John Chappell
Tom Clardy
Dick Collins
Stan Crooke
Jerry Cropp
Paul Curcio
Elliott Curson
Mitch Daniels

Tobey Dichter
Kit Donahue
Joe Drennan
George Ebright
Dick Evans
Blaine Fabian
Don Fair
Bill Farley
Rege Filtz
Ron Gidwitz
Steve Godomski
Linda Gohlke
Phil Goldsmith
Tom Griscom
Harry Groome
Bob Holland
Marc Holtzman
Tod Hullin
Jim Kerr
Graham King
Bob Kirkpatrick
Kathy Lamensdorf

Steve Lesnik
Jim Macaleer
Brian MacIntosh
Toby Maloney
Pat Marceante
Amy Margolis
Sam McCullough
Bill McDonough
Mary Mochary
Dan Molesky
Dennis Mollura
Bob Moser
Ed O'Brien
Dan Phelan
Kathy Phillips
Henry Pollak
Walt Reed
Elliot Richardson
George Roberts
Billie Rorres

Don Rumsfeld
Bob Shapiro
George Smith
Thym Smith
Sandy Spratt
Bob Stevens
Tom Stenzel
Jera Stribling
Pat Sylvester
Randy Thurman
Joanne Tracy
Frank Ursomarso
Catherine Votaw
George Westerman
Joe Westner
Gil Wetzel
Bernie Windon
Dick Wirthlin
Al Wolf
Rick Wooten

INDEX

Note: Page numbers in italics indicate illustrations.

A

Accuracy
  audience analysis and, 61
Accusing-questions, 5
Active listening, 29–31
Advantage
  stock issues of, 14
Adversarial situations
  special options for, 81–82
Agenda
  questioner's or respondent's,
    92–93
Amenities, 106–107
Anderson, John, 114
Anti-climax vs. climax approach, 88
Approachability, 52
Argument option, 82
Argument-presenting questions, 5
Aronson, Eliot, 52
Articulation, 45
Assumption dissection, 119
Attire, 46
Attitudinal analysis, 57
Audience analysis, 55–57
  making it work, 57–58
  obtaining information for, 59–61
  targeting of, 58–61
Audience attention, 73–74

Audience reluctance, 151–152
"Authority robbers," 44

B

Bad habits
  fixing, 28–29
Bakker, Jim, 41
Banana peels, 114–134. See also
    specific types
Basic-fact questions, 4
Biden, Joe, 41
"Blowing whistle," 104
Body language, 31–32
Boomerang effect, 26, 28, 99, 120
Bork, Robert, 55–56
*Bork Crusade Against Radicals and
    Leftists, The* (Kamen), 56
Brainstorming, 12
Bush, George, 53, 88–89, 145,
    200–201

C

Campanis, A1, 111–112, 113
Candor, 41–42
Carter, Jimmy, 26, 35, 99, 113, 114,
    136–137, 197

OTHER BOOKS BY
MYLES MARTEL

Political Campaign Debates: Images, Strategies, and Tactics
 Longman

Before You Say A Word: The Executive Guide to Effective Communication
 Prentice Hall

The Persuasive Edge: The Executive's Guide to Speaking and Media Appearances
 Random House
 Ballantine Books

FOR FURTHER INFORMATION

If you wish to receive free of charge any of the items listed below, please send a self-addressed stamped envelope to:

**Martel & Associates
One Aldwyn Center
Villanova, Pennsylvania 19085**

_____ "Combating Speech Anxiety," by Myles Martel
_____ "Expecting the Unexpected, Preparing for Crisis Situations," by Myles Martel
_____ "Guidelines for a Successful Speech or Presentation"
_____ Additional information regarding the services of Martel & Associates

NOTE: Please use two or more 25-cent stamps if you select more than two items.